X-MEN

W9-CPP-526

PHOENIX RISING

X-MEN

WRITERS
ROGER STERN, JOHN BYRNE, BOB LAYTON &
CHRIS CLAREMONT

PENCILERS
JOHN BUSCEMA, JOHN BYRNE, JACKSON GUICE,
JOHN BOLTON & MIKE COLLINS

INKERS
TOM PALMER, TERRY AUSTIN, BOB LAYTON,
JACKSON GUICE, JOSEF RUBINSTEIN
& JOHN BOLTON

COLORISTS
CHRISTIE SCHEELE, GLYNIS OLIVER,
PETRA SCOTESE & BOB SHAREN

LETTERERS
JIM NOVAK, JOHN WORKMAN, TOM ORZECHOWSKI
& JOE ROSEN

EDITORS
MARK GRUENWALD, MICHAEL CARLIN,
MICHAEL HIGGINS, ANN NOCENTI & BOB HARRAS

FRONT COVER ARTIST
JOHN BYRNE

FRONT COVER COLORS
TOM CHU

BACK COVER ARTIST
JOHN BOLTON

BACK COVER COLORS
CHRIS SOTOMAYOR

COLLECTION EDITOR
NELSON RIBEIRO

EDITORIAL ASSISTANTS
JOE HOCHSTEIN & JAMES EMMETT

ASSISTANT EDITOR
ALEX STARBUCK

EDITORS, SPECIAL PROJECTS
MARK D. BEAZLEY & JENNIFER GRÜNWALD

SENIOR EDITOR, SPECIAL PROJECTS
JEFF YOUNGQUIST

COLOR RECONSTRUCTION
JERRON QUALITY COLOR, USA DESIGN & TOM SMITH

PRODUCTION
JERRON QUALITY COLOR & JERRY KALINOWSKI

RESEARCH
JEPH YORK

SENIOR VICE PRESIDENT OF SALES
DAVID GABRIEL

SVP OF BRAND PLANNING & COMMUNICATIONS
MICHAEL PASCIULLO

EDITOR IN CHIEF
AXEL ALONSO

CHIEF CREATIVE OFFICER
JOE QUESADA

PUBLISHER
DAN BUCKLEY

EXECUTIVE PRODUCER
ALAN FINE

X-MEN: PHOENIX RISING. Contains material originally published in magazine form as AVENGERS #263, FANTASTIC FOUR #286, X-FACTOR #1, and CLASSIC X-MEN #8 and #43. Second edition. First printing 2011. ISBN# 978-0-7851-5786-1. Published by MARVEL WORLDWIDE, INC., a subsidiary of MARVEL ENTERTAINMENT, LLC. OFFICE OF PUBLICATION: 135 West 50th Street, New York, NY 10020. Copyright © 1986, 1987, 1990 and 2011 Marvel Characters, Inc. All rights reserved. $14.99 per copy in the U.S. and $16.99 in Canada (GST #R127032852); Canadian Agreement #40668537. All characters featured in this issue and the distinctive names and likenesses thereof, and all related indicia are trademarks of Marvel Characters, Inc. No similarity between any of the names, characters, persons, and/or institutions in this magazine with those of any living or dead person or institution is intended, and any such similarity which may exist is purely coincidental. **Printed in the U.S.A.** ALAN FINE, EVP - Office of the President, Marvel Worldwide, Inc. and EVP & CMO Marvel Characters B.V.; DAN BUCKLEY, Publisher & President - Print, Animation & Digital Divisions; JOE QUESADA, Chief Creative Officer; JIM SOKOLOWSKI, Chief Operating Officer; DAVID BOGART, SVP of Business Affairs & Talent Management; TOM BREVOORT, SVP of Publishing; C.B. CEBULSKI, SVP of Creator & Content Development; DAVID GABRIEL, SVP of Publishing Sales & Circulation; MICHAEL PASCIULLO, SVP of Brand Planning & Communications; JIM O'KEEFE, VP of Operations & Logistics; DAN CARR, Executive Director of Publishing Technology; SUSAN CRESPI, Editorial Operations Manager; ALEX MORALES, Publishing Operations Manager; STAN LEE, Chairman Emeritus. For information regarding advertising in Marvel Comics or on Marvel.com, please contact John Dokes, SVP Integrated Sales and Marketing, at jdokes@marvel.com. For Marvel subscription inquiries, please call 800-217-9158. **Manufactured between 7/27/2011 and 8/15/2011 by R.R. DONNELLEY, INC., SALEM, VA, USA.**

10 9 8 7 6 5 4 3 2 1

PHOENIX RISING

ALL MY FAULT

If you haven't read these stories yet, you might want to skip this introduction until you have — I'm going to talk about how the story came to be, and as such, I may end up spoiling surprises for new readers. That said, onward…

To call these stories controversial, when they first came out, would be an understatement. It had been five years since the X-Man known as Phoenix — Jean Grey, or so we thought — had sacrificed herself to save the universe from the inevitable threat of Dark Phoenix. And here was Marvel, telling readers that no, that wasn't quite Jean, and she'd really been alive all this time?

Some readers were pleased, of course, and glad to see Jean back. Others were horrified, feeling that to tamper with the story in which Phoenix died was to rob it of its power, and turn it into a travesty. "Who came up with this rotten idea?" they wanted to know.

Well, uh, me.

And here's how it came to be…

Back in 1980, while I was in college, some friends and I heard through the grapevine that Jean's death had been decreed, and would hit in *X-Men #137*. We didn't have the Internet back then, but news traveled fast — and we heard not only that Jim Shooter, editor-in-chief of Marvel back then, had demanded that Jean die for her acts as Dark Phoenix (specifically, killing the entire planet of D'Bari), but that he wouldn't allow any creators to resurrect her, unless some way could be found that left her not guilty of Dark Phoenix's crimes.

We were aghast — we were all fans of the original X-Men, and hated the idea of any of the original team being killed off. But in addition, we were intrigued by the caveat — that she couldn't come back unless she was innocent. We spent a fine evening talking comics, and working out possible scenarios for Jean's return — a return from a death we hadn't yet seen. My idea was that Phoenix hadn't really been Jean — but an incarnation of the Phoenix-force (something Chris Claremont had seemed to at least hint at when he made references to Phoenix being a separate entity from Jean) that had used Jean as a template to give itself form. Dark Phoenix, to my mind, was the inevitable corruption of the resulting entity as it grew further and further apart from its source. And that would mean Jean was still alive, cocooned at the bottom of Jamaica Bay.

Now mind you, this wasn't anything I intended to pitch to Marvel. It was just a creative exercise, a way for a few friends to have some fun, and vent our annoyance at a story we didn't like the sound of. I filed the story away in my mind, and that was that…or so I thought.

Three years later, I'd broken into the business — I was writing *Power Man and Iron Fist*, my first regular assignment, at the time — and was attending one of my first comics conventions as a pro. It was in Ithaca, New York, which meant I got to hang out with Roger Stern, a superb craftsman and all-around affable guy. Our chat turned to the X-Men, and at one point, Roger commented that he'd like to see Jean Grey return, but there was no way to do it without getting around Shooter's ruling on the matter.

"Sure there is," I said, snot-nosed young whippersnapper that I was.

I outlined the idea I'd come up with, and Roger liked it. Again, there was no thought of actually using it — it was just more comics conversation, and it ended there. Or so, once again, I thought.

BY KURT BUSIEK

was two years later or so that I was working as the assistant editor on *Marvel Age*, when Bob Layton breezed up to me in Marvel's bullpen and said, "Hey, I hear you're the guy I have to thank for saving Jean back!"

"Huh?" I responded brightly, having no idea what he was talking about.

It seems that in the intervening time, Roger had mentioned the idea to his pal John Byrne, and John had liked it, too. And when word got out that Bob would be doing a new series called *X-Factor*, reuniting the four surviving original X-Men, John called Bob and said, "I know a way you could have Jean in the team, too…"

So Bob ran the idea past Jim Shooter, and Jim okayed it. And Roger got to show Jean being found in *Avengers*, John got to revive her in *Fantastic Four*, and Bob got to reunite the original X-Men in *X-Factor #1*. Me, I got paid for the idea, got a credit line in Fantastic Four (even if my name was misspelled, rowr), and I got to edit the issue of *Marvel Age* that promoted the whole thing.

Now, you'll notice that I've cleverly taken all the credit for Jean's return (my idea! my idea!) and ducked all the blame (it wasn't me who decided to do it! I didn't even know it was happening!). But all I contributed, in the final analysis, was the idea — the explanation of how Jean could still be alive — and that wasn't a story. It was up to Roger (with John Buscema), John (with some uncredited revisions by Chris Claremont and Jackson Guice, the result of creative differences with the editor-in-chief that would soon see John departing *Fantastic Four*) and Bob Layton (with Guice again) to take that explanation and build an actual story around it. Which they did — and that's what you'll see in the pages that follow. A solid, dramatic, involving story, one that played a significant part in the ongoing history of the Marvel Universe — and which can now serve as a companion volume to *The Dark Phoenix Saga*, filling in latecomers who know, thanks to that volume, how Jean "died," but have never been sure just how she came back.

And that's it — the story of how an idea started out as idle conversation among a group of comics fans, and wound up becoming a reality. To all of you out there who think this story "ruined" *X-Men #137*, my apologies. For my part, I think Phoenix's sacrifice holds up pretty well as a powerful and affecting story, however much it annoyed me at the time of publication — and I'll admit, I do like the Marvel Universe a little better, knowing that Jean's still walking around in it.

But do me a favor, would you? If you ever come up with a great idea for how Uncle Ben or Bucky could still be alive... keep it to yourself, okay?

Kurt Busiek
February 1999

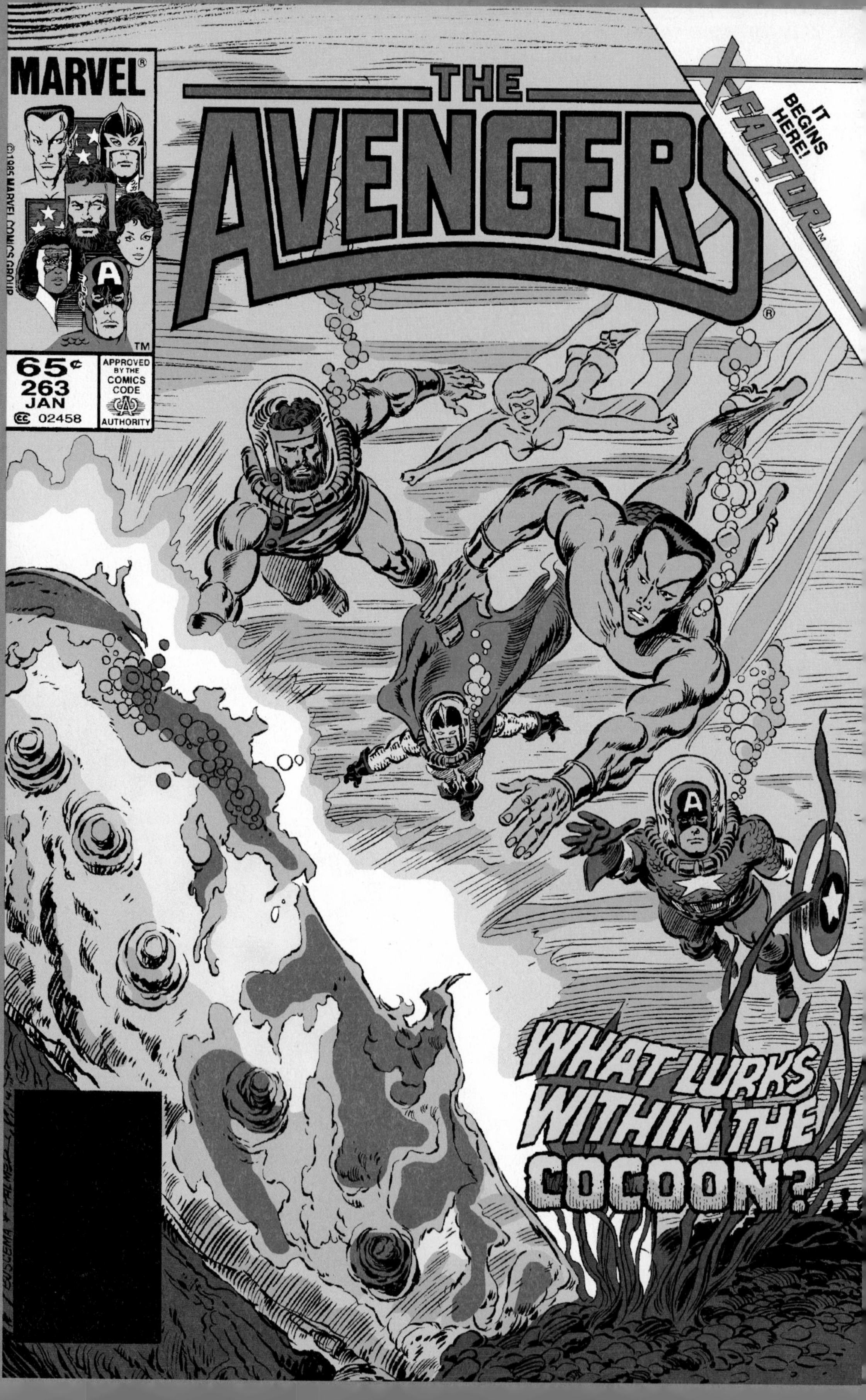

MARVEL®
THE AVENGERS®
X-FACTOR™
IT BEGINS HERE!
©1985 MARVEL COMICS GROUP
TM
65¢
263
JAN
02458
APPROVED BY THE COMICS CODE AUTHORITY
WHAT LURKS WITHIN THE COCOON?

JFK INTERNATIONAL AIRPORT...

TOWER, THIS IS CHARTER-AIR BETA-5-NINER... STILL WAITING CLEARANCE FOR *TAKEOFF.*

ROGER, BETA-5-NINER... JUST KEEP YOUR SHIRTS ON. WE'LL GET TO YOU.

"WE'LL GET TO YOU." I HATE BEING MADE TO *WAIT* LIKE COMMON RABBLE.

WILL YOU SHUT UP, *MORLAK?* ONCE OUR NEW PROJECT IS UNDERWAY, NO ONE WILL EVER BE ABLE TO MAKE YOU WAIT AGAIN!

IF WE CAN GET IT UNDERWAY, *ZOTA!*

DOUBTS FROM *YOU, SHINSKI?*

NOT ABOUT OUR ABILITY TO MAKE OUR PROJECT WORK... WE OF THE *ENCLAVE* POSSESS THE GREATEST *MINDS* ALIVE TODAY! THE CONTENTS OF THIS CRATE ALONE WILL MAKE US *MASTERS* OF THIS UNWORTHY WORLD!

NO, I AM AFRAID THAT WE WILL BE STOPPED BEFORE WE CAN REACH OUR *NEW RETREAT!*

YOUR FACES ARE ON *WANTED POSTERS* AROUND THE WORLD -- AND YOU WERE NONE TOO CAREFUL IN ACQUIRING THIS PLANE! WHAT IF YOU WERE *SPOTTED?*

WE HAVE BEEN KEPT WAITING HERE FAR LONGER THAN TRAFFIC WOULD REQUIRE. THE AUTHORITIES COULD BE CLOSING IN ON US EVEN NOW!

YOU'RE *PARANOID,* SHINSKI!

MAYBE NOT, ZOTA. *LOOK...*

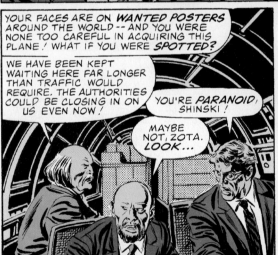

"...POLICE VANS! AND THEY'RE HEADED THIS WAY!"

"GET US OUT OF HERE, ZOTA! *NOW!*"

ROGER STERN
WRITER

JOHN BUSCEMA
BREAKDOWNS

TOM PALMER
FINISHER

JIM NOVAK
LETTERER

CHRISTIE SCHEELE
COLORIST

MARK GRUENWALD
EDITOR

JIM SHOOTER
EDITOR-IN-CHIEF

BETA-5-NINER--YOU ARE *NOT* CLEARED FOR TAKE OFF!

BETA-5-NINER, DO YOU *COPY*?

BETA-5--! FOR PETE'S SAKE, *STOP!*

YOU'RE HEADED RIGHT FOR A 747!!

DESPERATELY, ZOTA PULLS HIS JET INTO A SHARP, BANKING *TURN*, BUT...

KRRNNG

HOPELESSLY OUT OF CONTROL, THE PLANE SLAMS TO THE GROUND--SKIDDING ACROSS THE RUNWAY AND OUT INTO JAMAICA BAY!

IN SECONDS, THREE QUARTERS OF ITS RUPTURED HULL HAS SUNK BENEATH THE MURKY WATERS.

THIS IS AGENT FREEMAN! I WANT *AMBULANCES* AND A DREDGING CREW--AND I WANT 'EM NOW!

I'LL NEED *DIVERS*, TOO! THERE'S NO TELLING WHAT IS ABOARD THAT PLANE!

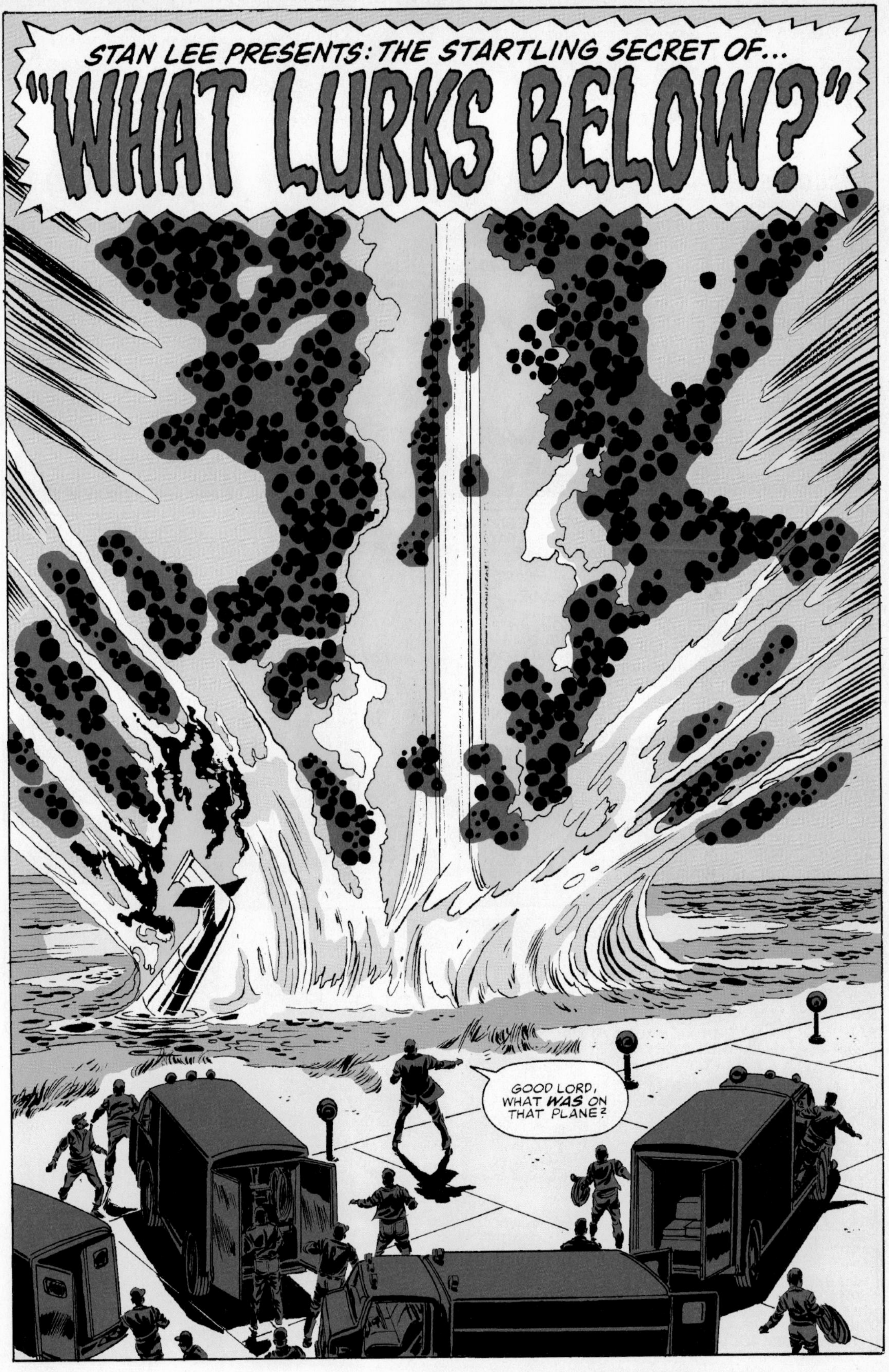
STAN LEE PRESENTS: THE STARTLING SECRET OF...
"WHAT LURKS BELOW?"
GOOD LORD, WHAT WAS ON THAT PLANE?

AT THAT MOMENT, IN THE FIFTH AVENUE HEADQUARTERS OF EARTH'S MIGHTIEST SUPER-TEAM...

TELL ME I HEARD YOU **WRONG!** TELL ME YOU DIDN'T JUST SAY THAT YOU INTEND TO MAKE THE **SUB-MARINER** AN AVENGER!

I DIDN'T **THINK** OUR GOVERNMENT LIASON WOULD TAKE THE NEWS TOO WELL!

I KNOW THAT NAMOR HASN'T ALWAYS BEEN ON THE **BEST OF TERMS** WITH THE SURFACE WORLD, MR. SIKORSKI... BUT HERE'S OUR CHANCE TO **CHANGE** THAT.

BUT, **CAP**...

THERE SHOULDN'T BE ANY PROBLEMS WITH **IMMIGRATION**... NAMOR'S FATHER WAS AN AMERICAN CITIZEN. AND HE **DID** DEFEND THESE SHORES DURING WORLD WAR II.

BUT...

MR. SIKORSKI, YOU KNOW THAT AS LONG AS OUR **SECURITY CLEARANCE** IS IN LIMBO, THE FEDERAL GOVERNMENT HASN'T ANY **SAY** IN WHAT WE DO! WE DIDN'T EVEN HAVE TO INFORM YOU OF OUR NEW MEMBER... BUT WE DID.

SCORE ONE FOR YOU, JAN!

THIS WON'T MAKE MY JOB ANY **EASIER**, WASP! I'VE BEEN WORKING FOR **WEEKS** TO FIND A WORKABLE FORMULA FOR RESTORING AVENGERS PRIORITY--!

WE APPRECIATE THAT, SIR. BUT I THINK NAMOR WILL WORK OUT.

YOU SEE? **CAPTAIN AMERICA** VOUCHES FOR THE **SUB-MARINER**. I'M SURE YOU HAVE NOTHING TO **WORRY** ABOUT!

FROM FIRM TO REASSURING IN LESS THAN A MINUTE...

...JANET VAN DYNE, YOU **ARE** A WONDER! I WONDER IF THERE'S ROOM ON YOUR CALENDER FOR DINNER WITH AN ADMIRING **BLACK KNIGHT**?

THREE LEVELS ABOVE...

AND **HERE**, NAMOR, BE THE PRIVATE QUARTERS OF AVENGERS-IN-RESIDENCE.

WHAT...OFF THIS COMMON HALL?

THE, UH, ROOMS ARE VERY **SPACIOUS**--

--AND CAN BE **DECORATED** TO YOUR LIKING!

WELL! SO I **SEE!**

THESE QUARTERS ARE INDEED NOTEWORTHY... SIMPLE, BUT WITH A CLASSIC ELEGANCE. YES, **THIS** WILL SUIT ME FINE, JUST AS IS!

NO DOUBT IT **WOULD**, WERE IT NOT ALREADY SPOKEN FOR NAMOR. 'TIS **MINE!**

AND I **LIKE** IT A GREAT DEAL, HERCULES. OF COURSE, YOU WOULDN'T MIND **SWITCHING** ROOMS!

YES, I **WOULD** MIND.

I'M SURE THAT--!

SEE **HERE**, HERCULES--!

NO, **YOU** SEE HERE--!

WITH A SHRUG OF RESIGNATION, **CAPTAIN MARVEL** TRANSFORMS HER PHYSICAL BODY INTO **PHOTONIC LIGHT**, AND...

I'VE ALREADY BROKEN UP **ONE** FIGHT BETWEEN THOSE TWO-- I DON'T FEEL LIKE MAKING A **CAREER** OUT OF IT!

I WONDER IF MAKING THE SUB-MARINER AN AVENGER WAS SUCH A GOOD IDEA. NAMOR CERTAINLY ISN'T GOING OUT OF HIS WAY TO *FIT IN.*

ATOP A HIGH TOWER, THE GOLDEN AVENGER WILLS HERSELF BACK TO HUMAN FORM...

MAYBE IT'S JUST *ME.*

NAMOR WAS *BORN* WITH THOSE INCREDIBLE AMPHIBIAN POWERS OF HIS, AND RAISED AS THE "AVENGING SON" OF ATLANTEAN ROYALTY. I SUPPOSE I CAN'T EXPECT HIM TO ACT LIKE THE *REST* OF US...

...BUT HE'D STILL BE A LITTLE EASIER TO TAKE IF HE DIDN'T ACT SO HIGH-AND-MIGHTY!

BACK HOME IN NEW ORLEANS, SUPER-BEINGS DON'T GET THE *MEDIA* COVERAGE THEY DO HERE IN NEW YORK--

--BUT EVEN SO, I'VE HEARD MORE THAN A FEW STORIES ABOUT THE SUB-MARINER... *NONE* OF THEM *FAVORABLE!*

OH, I'M PROBABLY WORRYING ABOUT NOTHING! AFTER ALL, *CAPTAIN AMERICA* NOMINATED NAMOR, AND I'VE NEVER HAD REASON TO DOUBT CAP'S JUDGMENT BEFORE, BUT...

...I DON'T KNOW THAT I *TRUST* THE SUB-MARINER.

JUST THEN...

WHAT ON EARTH--?!?

THAT PLUME OF ENERGY MUST HAVE SHOT A *MILE* OR MORE INTO THE SKY.

AND IT LOOKED TO BE COMING RIGHT FROM THE MIDDLE OF--

--JFK AIRPORT!

EXCUSE ME... I'M CAPTAIN MARVEL OF THE AVENGERS. ARE YOU IN CHARGE HERE? WHAT'S GOING ON?

UH...Y-YES. YES, I AM. AS TO WHAT'S GOING ON, I WISH I KNEW.

I'M *DEREK FREEMAN*, FBI. SOME FUGITIVES CRASHED INTO THE BAY DURING AN ATTEMPT TO AVOID CAPTURE... I BELIEVE YOU KNEW THEM AS THE *ENCLAVE.*

THE ENCLAVE?! YES, I WAS IN ON THEIR *FIRST* CAPTURE.* ARE THEY STILL ALIVE?

YES. THEY WERE IN PRETTY BAD SHAPE WHEN WE FISHED THEM OUT, BUT I THINK THEY'LL *LIVE.*

THEY'RE THE *LEAST* OF MY WORRIES NOW, THOUGH. I DON'T KNOW WHAT ALL CARGO THEY HAD IN THEIR PLANE, BUT AFTER IT SPILLED INTO THE BAY, THOSE ENERGY GEYSERS STARTED ERUPTING EVERY FEW MINUTES.

I SENT A COUPLE OF DIVERS DOWN JUST BEFORE THE LAST ONE. I HOPE THEY'RE ALL RIGHT.

AW, DON'T WORRY 'BOUT THOSE *TWO*, MR. FREEMAN! THEY'LL PROB'LY BE BREAKING THE SURFACE--

*AVENGERS ANNUAL #12.

FOOOSH

--ANY MINUTE NOW, I... HOLY GEEZ--!

NELSON, ARE YOU OKAY?

Y-YEAH, I THINK SO. HOW'S CARTER?

YOUR BUDDY HAD THE WIND KNOCKED OUT OF HIM, BUT HE'LL BE ALL RIGHT.

YOU TWO SHOT OUT OF THE WATER LIKE A COUPLE OF POLARIS MISSILES. WHAT HAPPENED DOWN THERE?

I'M NOT SURE. WE FOUND...SOMETHING. IT SEEMED TO BE THE SOURCE OF THAT CRAZY ENERGY. WHEN CARTER POKED IT WITH A PROBE, THERE WAS THIS VOICE...

...IT WASN'T LIKE ANY VOICE I'D EVER HEARD!

IT WARNED US TO KEEP AWAY. THEN, THE NEXT THING I KNEW, SOMETHING GRABBED US...AND THREW US OUT OF THE WATER!

I'D SAY THIS WAS OUT OF THE FBI'S LEAGUE, AGENT FREEMAN. I SUGGEST YOU CALL THE AVENGERS AT ONCE! TELL THEM I'M CHECKING THIS OUT!

WHEW.!! THAT'S ONE TAKE-CHARGE LADY!

THIS BAY'S A LOT *DEEPER* THAN IT LOOKS. MURKY DOWN HERE... BUT STILL, I'D BETTER HOLD MY LIGHT BACK TO *"LOW BEAMS"*--

--IF I WANT TO SNEAK UP ON THIS *WHATEVER-IT-IS.*

WELL, NOW! WHAT HAVE WE HERE? A BIG OL', BUSTED-UP *CRATE*--

--WITH WHAT LOOKS LIKE THE SHATTERED REMAINS OF SOME SORT OF HEAVY *GLASS TANK* INSIDE. BUT WAS IT SHATTERED ON IMPACT, OR DID SOMETHING *BREAK OUT?*

EH? THAT LIGHT'S NOT COMING FROM ME! WHERE--?

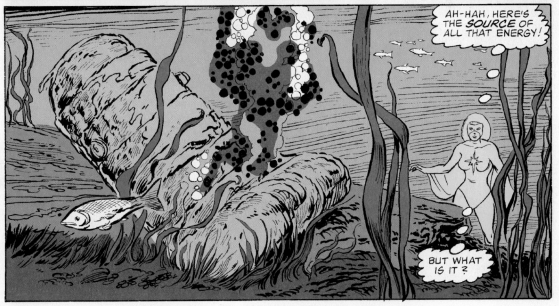

AH-HAH, HERE'S THE *SOURCE* OF ALL THAT ENERGY!

BUT WHAT IS IT?

WHATEVER IT IS, IT'S CERTAINLY A MESS! IT ALMOST LOOKS LIKE A COCOON FOR A GIANT-SIZED BUTTERFLY!

THAT LITTLE ENERGY CRACKLE IT'S EMITTING SEEMS TO BE ON THE WANE. MAYBE IT'S GROWING DORMANT.

WELL, WHATEVER IT'S DOING, I'LL FEEL A LOT BETTER AFTER I SEE WHAT'S UNDER THAT COVERING.

WITH A SINGLE, PRACTICED THOUGHT, CAPTAIN MARVEL TRANSFORMS HER LIGHT ENERGY--

--INTO A STREAM OF X-RAYS. BUT, AS THE SENTIENT RAYS TRY TO PIERCE THE SURFACE OF THE "COCOON", THEY MEET UNEXPECTED RESISTANCE.

NO...NO!

KEEP AWAY!

WH-WHAT IS THIS THING?! IT NOT ONLY REPELLED MY X-RAY BOMBARDMENT, IT'S TURNED ME PHYSICAL!

LEAVE ME ALONE!

THIS FORCE...IS KEEPING ME FROM CHANGING! AND IT'S NOT LETTING GO!

LEAVE... ME... ALONE!

BLASTED VOICE IS DRIVING ME CRAZY! G-GOT TO BREAK FREE ...OR I'LL DROWN.

CAN'T CONCENTRATE ENOUGH TO CHANGE. MUST... GET...

UHN? THE FORCE... IS WEAKENING.

...AWAY!

HOOWAAGH! ≋ KAUFF- KAUFF ≋

16

ELSEWHERE...

HAH-HA-HA! THAT'S IT, AVENGERS! FLY AWAY WHILE YOU CAN!

IDIOTS! IT WAS SO EASY TO TRAIN A SURVEILLANCE CAMERA ON YOUR FAMOUS MANSION!

I STILL DON'T SEE WHAT GOOD THAT CAMERA DOES US, MELTER!

THAT'S WHY YOU'LL NEVER BE MORE THAN HIRED MUS- CLE, KEEGAN! BUT I'LL EXPLAIN ONE MORE TIME! BY KEEPING WATCH LIKE THIS--

--I'LL BE ABLE TO TELL WHEN THE WHOLE TEAM HAS ASSEMBLED IN THE MANSION. WHEN I'M CERTAIN THAT THEY'RE ALL THERE, I'LL USE MY IMPROVED MELTING RAY TO DESTROY THEM-- MANSION AND ALL!

AFTER I'VE DESTROYED THE AVENGERS, NO ONE WILL EVER LAUGH AT THE MELTER AGAIN! ONCE I STRAP ON THE RAY PROJECTOR--

--I'LL BECOME TOTALLY... WHA--?

K-KEEGAN?!?

YES, MELTER...THAT'S THE REAL KEEGAN. I'VE GOT YOUR MELT- ING DEVICE RIGHT HERE!

BUT THAT'S NOT ALL I HAVE!

SPAK

PLIM

NEEYAKK!

JUSTICE IS SERVED!

KRUNK

17

WHILE, AT JFK...

THE *AVENGERS!* AWRIGHT, NOW WE'LL GET SOME *ACTION!*

HEY, TED...*DO YOU* SEE WHAT I SEE?

YEAH...THE *SUB-MARINER!* WHAT'S THAT *CREEP* DOIN' WITH THE AVENGERS?!

SHORTLY...

...AND THEN, THE DIVERS WADED IN AND HELPED ME TO SHORE.

MARVEL, YOU SAID THIS THING LOOKED LIKE AN OLD *MATTRESS* COVERED WITH *BARNACLES?*

YES...YOUR SKETCH IS VERY *CLOSE!*

I WAS *AFRAID* OF THAT. THIS ISN'T THE *FIRST* TIME THE ENCLAVE HAS CREATED SUCH A THING.

THE ENCLAVE HAS TRIED ON AT LEAST *TWO* PREVIOUS OCCASIONS TO GENETICALLY ENGINEER A RACE OF *SUPER-BEINGS*...BOTH TIMES INVOLVED COCOONS MUCH LIKE THE ONE YOU DESCRIBED!

*MARVEL TWO-IN-ONE #61.

**FANTASTIC FOUR #66-67.

"ACCORDING TO INFORMATION COMPILED BY THE FANTASTIC FOUR, THE MOST RECENT ATTEMPT YIELDED A MYSTERIOUS WOMAN KNOWN ONLY AS *HER**--BUT THEIR FIRST EXPERIMENT** CREATED THE MAN WHO BECAME *ADAM WARLOCK!*"

"BOTH HER AND WARLOCK REJECTED THE ENCLAVE'S ATTEMPTS TO SUBVERT THEIR WILLS. BUT THERE'S NO WAY OF KNOWING HOW THIS NEW BEING IS DEVELOPING DOWN THERE!"

YOU'RE RIGHT, CAP! WE COULD HAVE OUR HANDS *FULL* WITH THIS CREATURE. WE'D BETTER--!

THERE'S NOTHING TO *WORRY* ABOUT, WASP! THIS IS AN UNDERWATER MENACE-- I'LL HANDLE IT!

I WISH IT WERE THAT *SIMPLE*, NAMOR... BUT FIRST--! NAMOR?

NAMOR! COME BACK HERE!

OF ALL THE *NERVE*--!

HE IGNORED A DIRECT ORDER! WHEN WE GET BACK TO THE *MANSION*, I SAY WE BRING HIM UP ON *CHARGES*!

EASY, KNIGHT! SURE, NAMOR'S OUT OF LINE, BUT IT *HAS* BEEN A LONG TIME SINCE HE'S BEEN PART OF A *REAL TEAM!* HE'LL GET USED TO FOLLOWING ORDERS!

I HOPE YOU'RE RIGHT, CAP. ON SOMETHING AS *SERIOUS* AS THIS, WE CAN'T AFFORD ANY SCREW-

-UPS!

FOOSH

WHAT THE #$%&--?!?

19

WHY, MR. SUB-MARINER-- DON'T TELL ME YOU WERE THROWN OUT OF THE WATER BY THAT ITTY-BITTY *COCOON!*

I...

LOOK, I'LL SAY THIS *ONCE*...YOU CAN BE PART OF THE *TEAM,* OR YOU CAN *LEAVE!*

NICE OF YOU TO REJOIN US, NAMOR!

SAVE YOUR SARCASM, CAP. I KNOW WHEN I HAVE BEEN *HUMBLED.*

IN THE AVENGERS, WE WORK *TOGETHER,* NAMOR! REMEMBER THAT NEXT TIME, BEFORE YOU GO OFF HALF-COCKED!

MY ATOMIC STEED'S ALL READY TO GO! WHAT'S THE *PLAN?*

WE WERE JUST DISCUSSING THAT, DANE. THE ENCLAVERS MIGHT BE CONSCIOUS BY NOW, AND WILLING TO TALK. I COULD FLY TO THE HOSPITAL AND CHECK.

GOOD IDEA, C.M. IT WOULD HELP IF WE KNEW MORE ABOUT WHAT WE'RE UP AGAINST...HOW IT WAS CREATED ...WHAT *WEAK SPOTS* IT MIGHT HAVE!

AGREED. C.M., GO FIND OUT ALL YOU CAN, AS FAST AS YOU CAN!

AND WHAT OF THE *REST* OF US? ARE WE TO JUST STAND IDLY BY?

HARDLY! AS LONG AS THAT CREATURE IS ACTIVE DOWN THERE, WE DON'T HAVE THE LUXURY OF *WAITING!*

20

MOMENTS LATER... DOES EVERYBODY **READ** ME? LET'S HAVE A COMMUNICATIONS CHECK.

I READ YOU, WASP.

CHECK. LOUD AND CLEAR.

YES, MY RADIO **EAR-PLUG** ALLOWS ME TO HEAR YOU ALL QUITE WELL. I ASSUME MY **THROAT-MIKE** TRANSMITS AS CLEARLY.

AYE, NAMOR. BUT ENOUGH TALK... LEAD US TO THIS **BEAST!**

IT'S HARDLY A BEAST, HERCULES-- AT LEAST, NOT IN THE USUAL SENSE. THERE'S OUR QUARRY DEAD AHEAD.

ALL RIGHT, AVENGERS, YOU KNOW WHAT TO DO.

SLOWLY, CAUTIOUSLY, THE FIVE HEROES SURROUND THE EERIE COCOON...

THIS IS THE GREAT THREAT? IT'S LETTING US GET AWFULLY **CLOSE!**

ITS ENERGIES BUT **FLICKER** THROUGH A DOZEN RIPS AND TEARS. I CANNOT BELIEVE THAT THIS BESODDEN **LUMP** WAS RESPONSIBLE FOR--!

KEEP... AWAY!

NOW DO YOU BELIEVE, HERCULES?

BY MY BEARD, NONE SHALL SO THREATEN THE MIGHTY AVENGERS IN THE PRESENCE OF HERCULES!

NO!!

ZOUNDS!

HOLD ON, HERC! I'LL... HUH?

MY EBONY SWORD CAN DEFLECT ALL KINDS OF ENERGY, BUT IT'S NOT AFFECTING THESE POWER BLASTS AT ALL! WHAT IS THIS STUFF?

THE... SON... OF ZEUS... SHALL NOT BE... OVERCOME BY... COLORED LIGHTS!

HERCULES, THESE ARE NO MERE LIGHTS!

CAP, I CAN'T MOVE!

NEITHER CAN I, WASP!

KEEP BACK, DANE... NO SENSE OF US ALL BEING TRAPPED!

22

AT THAT MOMENT, MILES AWAY...

PROFESSOR SHINSKI? CAN YOU HEAR ME?

UHNN... WHO...?

I'M *CAPTAIN MARVEL*. YOU MUST HELP ME.

YOUR PARTNERS ARE STILL UNCONSCIOUS... AND YOUR CREATION IS LOOSE AT THE BOTTOM OF JAMAICA BAY. I CAN'T PROMISE ANYTHING, BUT IF YOU'LL TELL ME ALL ABOUT IT, THE COURTS MIGHT GO EASIER ON YOU.

CREATION?

WHAT... CREATION?

IN THE *COCOON*. I FOUND THE SHATTERED CRATE IT ESCAPED FROM.

YOUNG LADY... THERE WAS NO COCOON IN ANY CRATE. MY ASSOCIATES AND I WERE NEARLY *KILLED* BY PREVIOUS COCOON CREATURES... WE KNEW *BETTER* THAN TO TRY SUCH A THING AGAIN.

THERE WAS ONE CRATE... IT HELD MY NEW DISCOVERY IN A SPECIAL GLASS TANK. EVEN IF THE CRATE AND TANK WERE SHATTERED... THERE'D BE NO THREAT.

IN THOSE WATERS, THE NEW *COMPOUNDS* WOULD BE RENDERED INERT... *HARMLESS*...

HE'S LOST CONSCIOUSNESS AGAIN. I'M SURE HE WAS TELLING THE *TRUTH* -- HE WAS TOO OUT-OF-IT TO HAVE LIED.

BUT IF THE ENCLAVERS DIDN'T MAKE THAT THING, WHERE *DID* IT COME FROM?!

23

WHILE...

BAH! 'MIDST ALL THIS MUCK AND MIRE, 'TIS A *BATTLE* JUST TO GET *FOOTING!* BUT YET SHALL I OVERPOWER THIS FORCE!

HE'S DOING IT! THE OLYMPIAN IS ACTUALLY MAKING HEADWAY AGAINST THIS CRUSHING FORCE, WHILE I STAND *HELPLESS* IN ITS POWER!

HOW MUCH MORE MUST I BE HUMBLED?!

LISTEN UP, AVENGERS-- THIS FORCE BOLT SEEMS TO STOP ONLY MY *FORWARD* MOVEMENTS! AS I FALL BACK, ITS POWER *FADES OUT!*

SAME HERE, CAP! BACK OFF, EVERYBODY!

THERE BE NO NEED FOR MY RETREAT, WASP! INCH BY INCH, I *GAIN* 'PON THIS CURSED THING!

AS THE LION OF OLYMPUS LURCHES ANOTHER STEP FORWARD--

--THE SOURCE OF THE WILD ENERGIES IS SLOWLY FORCED BACK...

LOOK! THE COCOON IS SHEDDING A COAT OF *SILT* AS IT MOVES! IT'S *COVERED* WITH THE STUFF--

24

--BUT THE DEBRIS FROM THE *PLANE* IS STILL *CLEAN!*

OF COURSE, I SHOULD HAVE NOTICED SOONER! IT TAKES TIME FOR *THAT* MUCH SILT TO SETTLE ON AN OBJECT!

THEN THE COCOON COULDN'T HAVE COME FROM THE PLANE!

THAT *CONFIRMS* WHAT I'VE LEARNED. PROFESSOR SHINSKI CLAIMS THAT THE ENCLAVE HAD *NOTHING* TO DO WITH IT!

THEN WE'RE BACK TO SQUARE ONE. WHAT *IS* THIS THING?

WHAT IT IS MATTERS NOT! HERCULES SHALL O'ER-COME IT!

BUT, AS THE MAN-GOD CLOSES IN ON HIS TARGET...

NO... NO, *PLEASE!* GET BACK... STAY AWAY!

HAH! 'TIS WEAKENING!

HERCULES, YOU BIG LUNK, CAN'T YOU HEAR? IT'S *AFRAID!*

BACK OFF!

AND AS HERCULES HALF-TURNS TOWARD HIS GROUP'S LEADER, HE LOSES HIS FOOTING AND...

ZEUS--!!

CAP, COULD THIS THING HAVE JUST BEEN REACTING TO BEING *JOSTLED* AND *PROBED*--?

AND BEEN ACTING IN *SELF-DEFENSE?* THAT'S A DISTINCT POSSIBILITY, YES!

THEN WE HAVE TO CONVINCE IT THAT WE MEAN NO HARM. EVERYBODY STAY BACK.

THAT WEIRD VOICE WAS SOME SORT OF MENTAL PROJECTION...CAN IT "HEAR" ME AS WELL? MAYBE IF I *CONCENTRATE*--!

HELLO? WE WON'T HURT YOU...WE WANT TO HELP!

HELP?

JAN, *NO!*

HOLD IT, DANE--

--I THINK SHE'S *ONTO* SOMETHING!

YES, WE'LL DO ALL WE CAN.

H-HELP... HELP... ME...

AVENGERS, COME HERE--BUT *SLOWLY!*

HELLO, CAN YOU HEAR ME?

NO USE...THE VOICE FADED AWAY AS THAT CRACKLING ENERGY DISAPPEARED. THIS OUTER COVER PEELS OFF LIKE OLD ROTTED *FABRIC.* I WONDER...

WHAT IN THE WORLD IS *THIS?!*

SO, ONE MYSTERY UNLOCKS TO SHOW YET *ANOTHER.* YOU'VE FOUND US A CHINESE PUZZLE!

LET'S HOPE IT'S *SOLVABLE,* NAMOR!

SHORTLY, BACK AT AVENGERS MANSION... SO, SIR KNIGHT, WHAT MANNER OF BEAST *IS* THIS?

I WISH I HAD AN *ANSWER,* HERCULES. THE OUTER COVERING WAS JUST PART OF SOME OLD MATTRESS. THE THINGS THAT GET DUMPED IN THAT BAY--!

ANYWAY, THE CAPSULE ITSELF IS SOMETHING LIKE A *STASIS FIELD,* BUT IT DOESN'T *BEHAVE* LIKE ANY I'VE EVER ENCOUNTERED.

AND YOU HAVEN'T HEARD ANY MORE OF THAT *VOICE?*

NOT A PEEP. THERE HASN'T BEEN A SINGLE *LIFE-SIGN.* IT'S AS IF IT SWITCHED ITSELF *OFF.* IF ONLY WE KNEW WHERE IT CAME FROM!

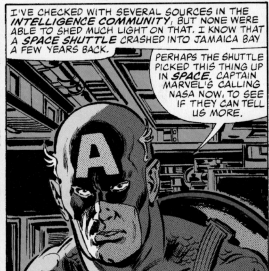

I'VE CHECKED WITH SEVERAL SOURCES IN THE *INTELLIGENCE COMMUNITY,* BUT NONE WERE ABLE TO SHED MUCH LIGHT ON THAT. I KNOW THAT A *SPACE SHUTTLE* CRASHED INTO JAMAICA BAY A FEW YEARS BACK.

PERHAPS THE SHUTTLE PICKED THIS THING UP IN *SPACE.* CAPTAIN MARVEL'S CALLING NASA NOW, TO SEE IF THEY CAN TELL US MORE.

SUDDENLY, OVER THE INTER-COM... NASA DOESN'T KNOW ANYTHING ABOUT OUR MYSTERY CAPSULE, CAP--

--BUT THE AIRPORT ADMINISTRATORS ARE ON THE LINE! THEY WANT US TO COORDINATE MOP-UP OPERATIONS WITH AGENT FREEMAN... JUST IN CASE THERE ARE ANY MORE SURPRISES!

THAT SHOULDN'T TAKE *ALL* OF US! OH, WELL... TRANSFER THE CALL TO THE *MAIN ASSEMBLY,* C.M.

WILL DO!

THE LABORATORY DOOR WHISPERS **SHUT** BEHIND THE AVENGERS, LOCKING THE MYSTERIOUS CAPSULE AWAY FROM SIGHT.

THERE IS NO ONE TO OBSERVE THE **POWER** THAT SURGES FROM DEEP WITHIN THE OPAQUE CAPSULE, TURNING IT FIRST TRANSLUCENT--

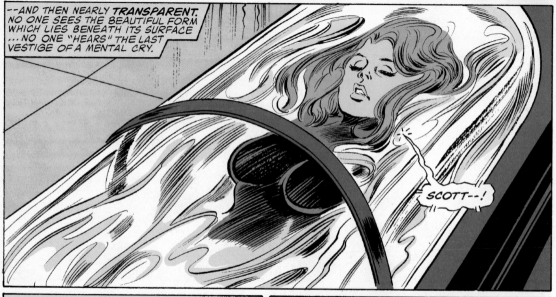

--AND THEN NEARLY **TRANSPARENT.** NO ONE SEES THE BEAUTIFUL FORM WHICH LIES BENEATH ITS SURFACE ...NO ONE "HEARS" THE LAST VESTIGE OF A MENTAL CRY.

SCOTT--!

IN SECONDS, THE POWER FADES. THE CAPSULE AGAIN GROWS OPAQUE... AND **SILENT.**

AND THE YOUNG WOMAN THE WORLD ONCE KNEW AS **JEAN GREY** IS ONCE MORE HIDDEN FROM THE WORLD.

OUR STORY CONTINUES IN FANTASTIC FOUR #286 ...ON SALE ONE WEEK FROM NOW! WHATEVER YOU DO, DON'T MISS...

"...LIKE A PHOENIX!"

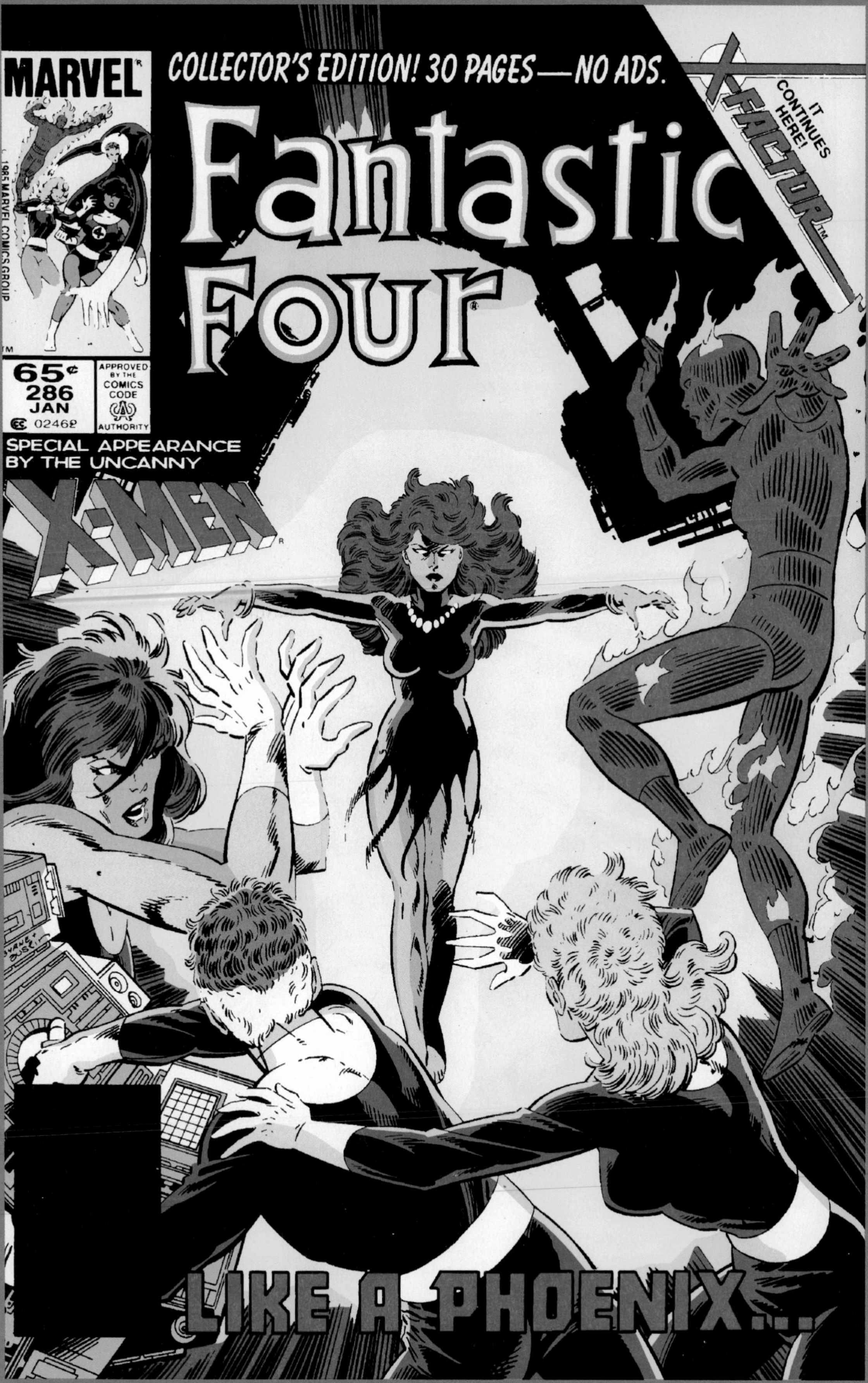
MARVEL
COLLECTOR'S EDITION! 30 PAGES—NO ADS.
Fantastic Four
X-FACTOR
IT CONTINUES HERE!
65¢
286
JAN
02462
APPROVED BY THE COMICS CODE AUTHORITY
©1985 MARVEL COMICS GROUP
SPECIAL APPEARANCE BY THE UNCANNY
X-MEN
LIKE A PHOENIX...

STAN LEE PRESENTS | YOU KNOW WHO WRITER/PENCILER | TERRY AUSTIN GUEST INKER | GLYNIS OLIVER COLORIST | JOHN WORKMAN LETTERER | MICHAEL CARLIN EDITOR | JIM SHOOTER EDITOR IN CHIEF | WITH SPECIAL THANKS TO R. STERN & K. BUSEK

LIKE A PHOENIX!

"EVERY PARTING GIVES A FORE-TASTE OF DEATH, EVERY COMING TOGETHER AGAIN A FORETASTE OF THE RESURRECTION."
A. SCHOPENHAUR (1788-1860 "STUDIES IN PESSIMISM"

THERE SHE IS! TERRA FIRMA! MOTHER EARTH!

THERE'VE BEEN TIMES IN THE PAST FEW WEEKS WHEN I BEGAN TO WONDER IF WE'D *EVER* SEE HER AGAIN!

REALLY NOW, SHE-HULK, YOU MAKE IT SOUND AS IF OUR EVENTUAL HOMECOMING WAS *UNLIKELY!*

WELL... NOT *"UNLIKELY"* EXACTLY, REED. IT JUST SEEMED TO GET FURTHER AND FURTHER AWAY...

...WHAT WITH ONE *DETOUR* AFTER ANOTHER!

BY NOW YOU SHOULD KNOW REED WELL ENOUGH TO REALIZE HE'S INTELLECTUALLY INCAPABLE OF PASSING BY ANYTHING OF THE *SLIGHTEST* COSMOLOGICAL INTEREST.

BUT... THAT'S ONE OF THE REASONS I *LOVE* HIM AS MUCH AS I DO!

SUE...

WELL, IF NOTHING ELSE, AT LEAST SOME OF THE LITTLE SIDE TRIPS WE TOOK ON THE WAY BACK SHOULD PROVIDE GRIST FOR SOME FINE *STORIES* FOR THE PEOPLE WHO PUBLISH OUR MAGAZINE.

MAYBE. LAST TIME I HEARD, THERE WAS A THEORY OVER THERE THAT "COSMIC DOESN'T SELL."

AND YOU CAN'T GET MUCH *MORE* COSMIC THAN THE LAST FEW WEEKS.

MAYBE NOT, TORCHIE...

BUT I'LL JUST BET THE F.F.'S LEGION OF *FANS* WOULD BE MIGHTY PEEVED IF THEY THOUGHT THEY WEREN'T GETTING *ALL* THE STORIES.

HEY, SHULKIE, A LOT OF THE STUFF WE GET INTO DOESN'T EVEN MAKE IT ONTO THE SIX O'CLOCK NEWS, NEVER MIND FAN MAGAZINES.

OKAY, KEEP IT DOWN A MINUTE NOW, YOU TWO.

I'M GOING TO CONTACT J.F.K.* FOR CLEARANCE TO LAND.

*JOHN F. KENNEDY INTERNATIONAL AIRPORT, NEW YORK.

REED RICHARDS CALLING KENNEDY FLIGHT CONTROL. REQUESTING CLEARANCE TO LAND.

REPEAT, THIS IS REED RICHARDS OF THE FANTASTIC FOUR CALLING J.F.K.

J.F.K. FLIGHT CONTROL TO REED RICHARDS.

CLEARANCE DENIED. REPEAT, CLEARANCE DENIED.

WE ARE CLOSED TO ALL INCOMING TRAFFIC UNTIL FURTHER NOTICE.

DIVERT TO LA GUARDIA, FANTASTIC FOUR.

RICHARDS TO KENNEDY. IS EVERYTHING ALL RIGHT?

CAN WE BE OF ANY ASSISTANCE?

NEGATIVE. EVERYTHING IS UNDER CONTROL NOW.

THE AVENGERS ARE HERE FINISHING WITH THE MOPPING UP.

THE AVENGERS! HUH! FIGURES MY OL' TEAMMATES WOULDN'T HAVE BEEN SITTING ON THEIR HANDS WHILE WE'VE BEEN STAR-HOPPING.

REED, MAYBE WE SHOULD HEAD STRAIGHT BACK TO HEADQUARTERS AND FIND OUT WHAT'S BEEN GOING ON?

IF WE WERE BOUND FOR THE OLD BAXTER BUILDING, I'D SAY FINE, SUE. BUT AVENGER'S MANSION* ISN'T EQUIPPED FOR A VEHICLE OF THIS SIZE TO LAND.

OUR BEST PLAN WILL BE TO LAND AT LA GUARDIA AND TAKE A TAXI OVER TO MANHATTAN AS QUICKLY AS WE CAN...

*WHERE THE F.F. HAVE BEEN STAYING SINCE THE DESTRUCTION OF THEIR H.Q.

NO, REALLY, MISTER FANTASTIC! TH' NUMBRA TIMES YOUSE GUYS'VE SAVED THIS TOWN... I JUST COULDN'T TAKE NO FARE.

WE DON'T MIND PAYING, SIR. THE FANTASTIC FOUR ALWAYS MEETS ITS DEBTS...

LET IT GO, REED. WE GOT OTHER FISH TO FRY.

YEH--LIKE FINDING OUT WHAT THE AVENGERS HAVE BEEN UP TO WITHOUT US!

WELL, WELL!!

LOOK WHO'S HERE!

REED! SUE! JOHNNY!

AND SHE-HULK, TOO! YOU'RE BACK.

GOOD TO SEE YOU.

VERILY, 'TIS ALWAYS GOOD TO SET EYES UPON TWO MAIDS SO FAIR OF FACE AND FORM,

CAPTAIN AMERICA, HERCULES... WE DIDN'T EXPECT TO FIND YOU HERE. WE THOUGHT SOMETHING WAS TRANSPIRING OVER AT J.F.K.

JAMAICA BAY, TO BE PRECISE, REED. THE WASP IS LEADING THE CLEAN-UP OPERATIONS OVER THERE.

AFRAID YOU MISSED MOST OF THE FIREWORKS THIS TIME...*

MOST... BUT NOT ALL, CAP?

WHAT'S BEEN HAPPENING?

T'WAS NOTHING, REED RICHARDS. A TRIFLING DISTRACTION FOR SUCH AS WOULD ALLY THEMSELVES WITH THE SON OF ZEUS!

*SURE HOPE YOU DIDN'T MISS AVENGERS #263.

33

"WELL, PERHAPS **MORE** THAN A **TRIFLING** DISTRACTION, HERCULES.

"IT BEGAN WITH THE **CRASH** OF A PRIVATE JET OUT AT J.F.K.

"A PLANE MAKING AN UNAUTHORIZED TAKE-OFF WITH AN UNAUTHORIZED CARGO.

"THE PLANE HAD HARDLY BEEN IN THE WATER A MOMENT WHEN A BOLT OF TREMENDOUS ENERGY BURST FROM THE WATERS.

"NATURALLY, WE **AVENGERS** INVESTIGATED, AND FOUND OURSELVES FACE-TO-FACE WITH A **MYSTERY.**

"THE OBJECT WAS COVERED IN SLIME AND SILT FROM THE BOTTOM OF THE BAY...

"...BUT IT WAS STILL GENERATING ENOUGH POWER TO GIVE US QUITE A ROUGH RIDE FOR A WHILE,

"EVENTUALLY, HOWEVER, WE **PREVAILED.**"

✱ FOR THE FULL STORY, PICK UP *AVENGERS* #263.

AND THE **BOTTOM LINE** IS, WE FOUND **THIS.**

SOMETHING THAT APPEARS TO HAVE HAD **NOTHING** TO DO WITH THAT PRIVATE JET, OR ITS PASSENGERS.

!?!

34

IT'S COMPLETELY *PLACID* JUST NOW-- SENSORS SHOW NO ACTIVITY ON ANY MEASURABLE ENERGY LEVELS.

BUT IT WAS PRETTY *HAIRY* FOR A WHILE THERE.

AMAZING!

I'VE NEVER SEEN ANYTHING QUITE LIKE...

UHNGH!

REED!

EASY, BABY BROTHER. I'M NOT ABOUT TO LET MY HUSBAND GET SPLATTERED.

AN *INVISIBLE FORCE-FIELD CUSHION* SHOULD DO THE TRICK.

Oomf!

QUICK THINKING, SUE, DARLING. THAT *NEURAL-SHOCK WAVE* TENSED EVERY VOLUNTARY MUSCLE IN MY BODY TO ROCK-LIKE RIGIDITY.

I HAD NO WAY OF USING MY ELASTIC POWERS TO SAVE MYSELF FROM INJURY.

BUT...REED, WHAT IN THE WORLD *IS* THAT THING?

NOTHING FROM *THIS* WORLD, I SUSPECT.

SUE, YOUR POWERS INCLUDE THE ABILITY TO MAKE OBJECTS *INVISIBLE*. LET'S SEE IF YOU CAN SHOW US THE *INSIDE* OF THAT THING.

ALL RIGHT...

BUT I DON'T GUARANTEE ANYTHING. THAT... OBJECT ALMOST LOOKS AS IF IT ISN'T REALLY THERE AT ALL!

THAT'S IT, SUE!

YOU'RE *GETTING* IT!

SOMETHING IS STARTING TO *APPEAR*...

BUT... I FEEL SOME KIND OF... *FEEDBACK*, AS IF THE OBJECT IS *RESISTING* MY *PROBE*.

TRY TO HOLD IT JUST A FEW SECONDS LONGER.

WE'VE ALMOST GOT A CLEAR VIEW OF THE INTERIOR OF THE...

GOOD LORD!!

IT'S... A *WOMAN*! A *HUMAN* WOMAN!!

Panel 1:

Oh-hhh!

SUE!! IT'S ALL RIGHT, MY LOVE! YOU CAN RE-LAX NOW!

WE'VE SEEN WHAT WE NEEDED TO SEE.

Panel 2:

BUT...WHO *IS* YON MAIDEN? IS SHE KNOWN TO ANY HERE?

NOT ME... BUT THEN I'M STILL *NEW* AT THIS.

SHE DID NOT LOOK AT ALL FAMILIAR TO ME, EITHER, SHE-HULK. CLEARLY, THIS WILL RE-QUIRE *INTENSIVE* RE-SEARCH.

Panel 3:

HO, WHOA! MY *BOREDOM-SENSE* JUST WENT OFF! THIS IS THE PART WHERE YOU GET INCREDIBLY *FO-CUSED* FOR ABOUT TWELVE DAYS...

...WHILE THE REST OF US STAND AROUND LIKE *ZOMBIES*, RIGHT?

WELL, I MIGHT HAVE CHOSEN A MORE...EN-LIGHTENED PHRASE-OLOGY, JOHNNY, BUT... YES, THAT IS ESSEN-TIALLY *IT!*

Panel 4:

WELL, FINE. I'LL TAKE THAT AS MY CUE TO SKEEDAD-DLE OUT OF HERE. I'VE GOT A LOVE-LY LADY WAITING FOR ME, AND IT'S BEEN TOO LONG SINCE I'VE BEEN WITH HER.

YOU KNOW WHERE TO FIND ME IF THE PLOT THICKENS.

YOU KNOW, THAT SOUNDS LIKE A GOOD PLAN, TORCHIE. I COULD USE A LITTLE HEAVY-DUTY HOME-COMING WITH THE LOVE OF MY OWN LIFE.

Panel 5:

HOW'S IT GOIN' WITH YOU AND MY OL' COL-LEGE ROOMIE, SHULKIE? I THOUGHT YOU AND WYATT WERE A PRETTY *HOT* ITEM, BUT AFTER THAT LITTLE NUM-BER WITH HERC...

SELF-DEFENSE, JOHNNY.

HERCULES HAS A TENDENCY TO PUT THE MAKE ON ANYTHING THAT HASN'T BEEN *CREMATED.*

I HAD TO COME UP WITH A LITTLE GAME PLAYING TO KEEP FROM GETTING SERI-OUS ABOUT HIM.

Panel 6:

ABOUT *HERCULES?* WHAT ARE YOU, INTO *OLDER MEN* OR SOMETHING?

WELL, THAT'S *PART* OF IT. I MEAN, THAT'S NOT SOME CIRCUS STRONG MAN WHO DECIDED TO CALL HIMSELF HERCULES. HE'S THE *REAL* HERCULES, FIVE THOUSAND YEARS OLD AND ALL!

THINK ABOUT IT, JOHNNY. THIS IS A MAN WHOSE *NAME* HAS BECAME AN *ADJECTIVE*, A PART OF THE LANGUAGE!

THAT'S A PRETTY TOUGH ACT FOR A GIRL TO WALK AWAY FROM.

AND ANYWAY ...MAYBE YOU DIDN'T NOTICE, BUT HE HAS *EYES* JUST LIKE *TOM SELLECK.*

GOOD MORNING, GENTLEMEN. I THOUGHT YOU MIGHT BE READY FOR A PICK-ME-UP.

JARVIS! YOU'RE A LIFE-SAVER!

BUT... WHAT ARE YOU DOING STILL UP? EVEN THE AVENGERS' *BUTLER* MUST NEED *SOME* REST!

ABOUT SIX HOURS A NIGHT, SIR.

WHICH I HAVE *HAD*, WHILE YOU'VE BEEN WORKING.

WHAT...? GREAT DAY, LOOK AT THE TIME!

WE'VE BEEN AT IT *EIGHT HOURS*, WITHOUT A BREAK!

AM 6:13

I TRUST YOU HAVE AT LEAST HAD A *FRUITFUL* NIGHT OF IT, MASTER REED?

WE'LL KNOW IN A FEW MINUTES, JARVIS.

WE'VE MANAGED TO LOCK ONTO A VERY SUBDUED *BRAINWAVE PATTERN*. WHOEVER THAT YOUNG LADY IS, SHE'S IN SOMETHING VERY CLOSE TO *SUSPENDED ANIMATION*.

ONLY HER *DEEPEST UN-CONSCIOUS MIND* IS EVEN *SLIGHTLY* ACTIVE, AND IT SEEMS TO BE *THAT* WHICH TRIGGERS THE DEFENSIVE EN-ERGIES OF THE... POD.

Ahh! THEN I TAKE IT YOU DO NOT FEEL THE YOUNG LADY HERSELF HAS SUPER-HUMAN POWERS?

I HON-ESTLY DON'T KNOW.

BUT THIS NEXT STEP INVOLVES A GENTLE *BIO-RADIANT* STIMULATION OF HER *CONSCIOUS MIND*.

HOPEFULLY WE CAN BRING HER OUT OF THE COMA-LIKE STATE, AND OUT OF THE POD...

I SEE, SIR. I...

...oh!

MASTER REED!!

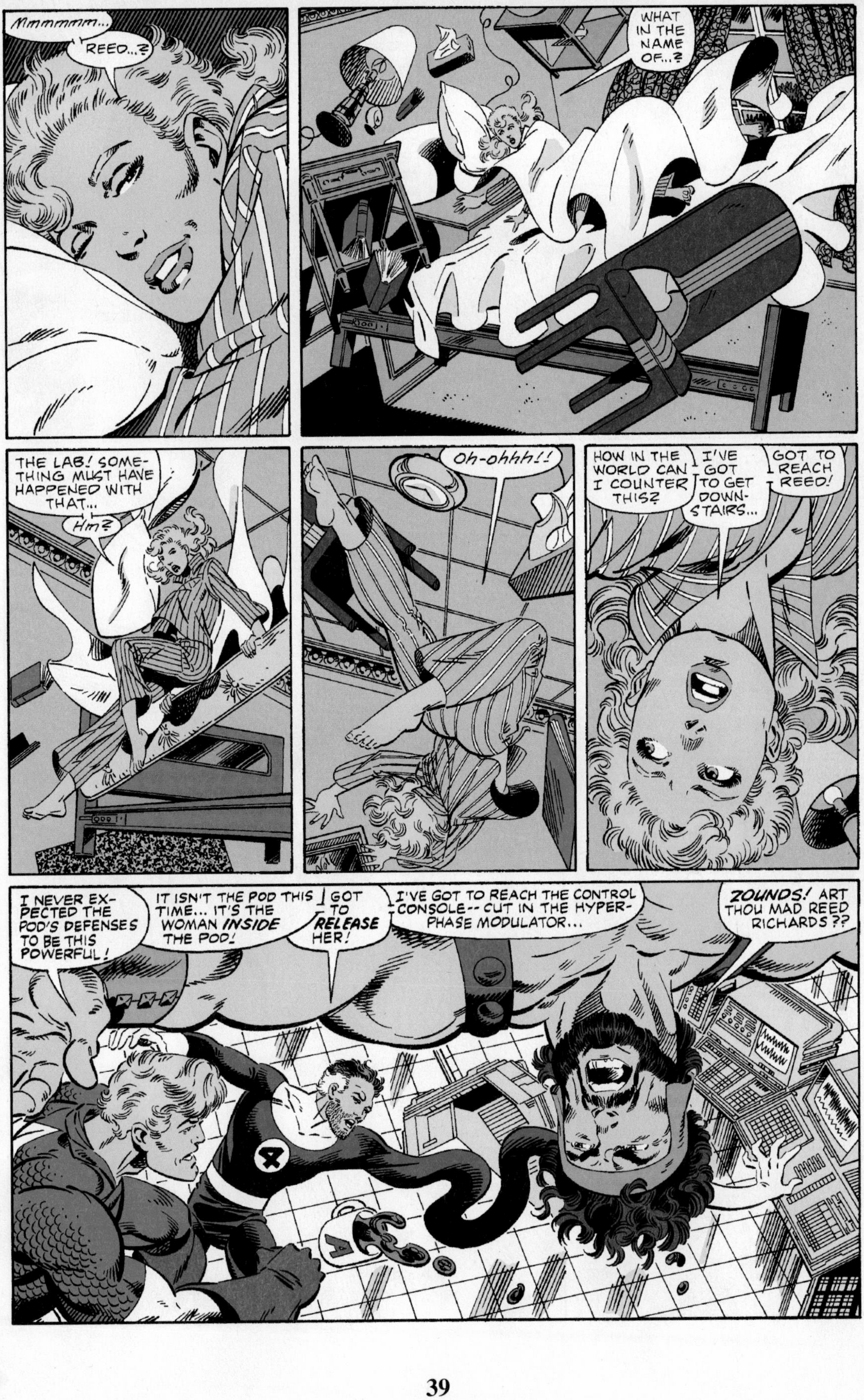
Mmmmmm...
REED...?
WHAT IN THE NAME OF...?
THE LAB! SOMETHING MUST HAVE HAPPENED WITH THAT...
Hm?
Oh-ohhh!!
HOW IN THE WORLD CAN I COUNTER THIS?
I'VE GOT TO GET DOWNSTAIRS...
GOT TO REACH REED!
I NEVER EXPECTED THE POD'S DEFENSES TO BE THIS POWERFUL!
IT ISN'T THE POD THIS TIME... IT'S THE WOMAN INSIDE THE POD!
GOT TO RELEASE HER!
I'VE GOT TO REACH THE CONTROL CONSOLE-- CUT IN THE HYPER-PHASE MODULATOR...
ZOUNDS! ART THOU MAD REED RICHARDS??

NOT AT ALL, HERCULES, JUST LOGICAL! CLEARLY JARVIS GUESSED CORRECTLY WHEN HE SUGGESTED THE WOMAN HERSELF MIGHT HAVE SUPER-POWERS.

NOW THAT THOSE POWERS ARE THEMSELVES FUNCTIONING THERE IS A GREAT DANGER THAT THE POD'S OWN DEFENSE MECHANISMS MAY TURN ON HER-- *DESTROYING HER!* UNLESS WE RELEASE HER FIRST!

OH, MY GOODNESS...

LOOK AT THE POD!!

WHAT'S HAPPENING TO IT?!?

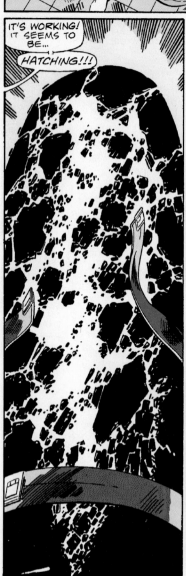

IT'S WORKING! IT SEEMS TO BE...

HATCHING!!!

YOUR ROTTEN LITTLE GAME IS *FINISHED*, LANG, YOUR SO-CALLED X-SENTINELS ARE FALLING APART.

NOW IT'S YOUR...

...TURN...?

YOU...YOU'RE NOT LANG, AND THIS DOESN'T LOOK LIKE THE S.H.I.E.L.D. SATELLITE...?

NOR WOULD I EXPECT IT TO, MISS.

THIS IS AVENGERS MANSION, AND I AM REED RICHARDS,

...OF THE FANTASTIC FOUR?

NOT EVEN CLOSE, PAL. THE LAST TIME I MET THEM, THE FF WORE BLUE COSTUMES...

...NOT BLACK!

WELL, THERE IS AN EXPLANATION, I ASSURE YOU.

IF YOU'D JUST LET US ALL DOWN...?

YES...THAT'S JUST WHAT YOU'D LIKE ME TO DO, ISN'T IT?

WELL, IT SEEMS TO ME IF STEPHEN LANG CAN BUILD DUPLICATES OF THE X-MEN, HE CAN DO THE SAME FOR ANYONE ELSE, RIGHT?

SO, AS LONG AS I SEEM TO HAVE ALL THIS EXTRA POWER, YOU BOYS CAN JUST KEEP BOUNCING AGAINST THE CEILING UNTIL...

UNGH!!

BOP!

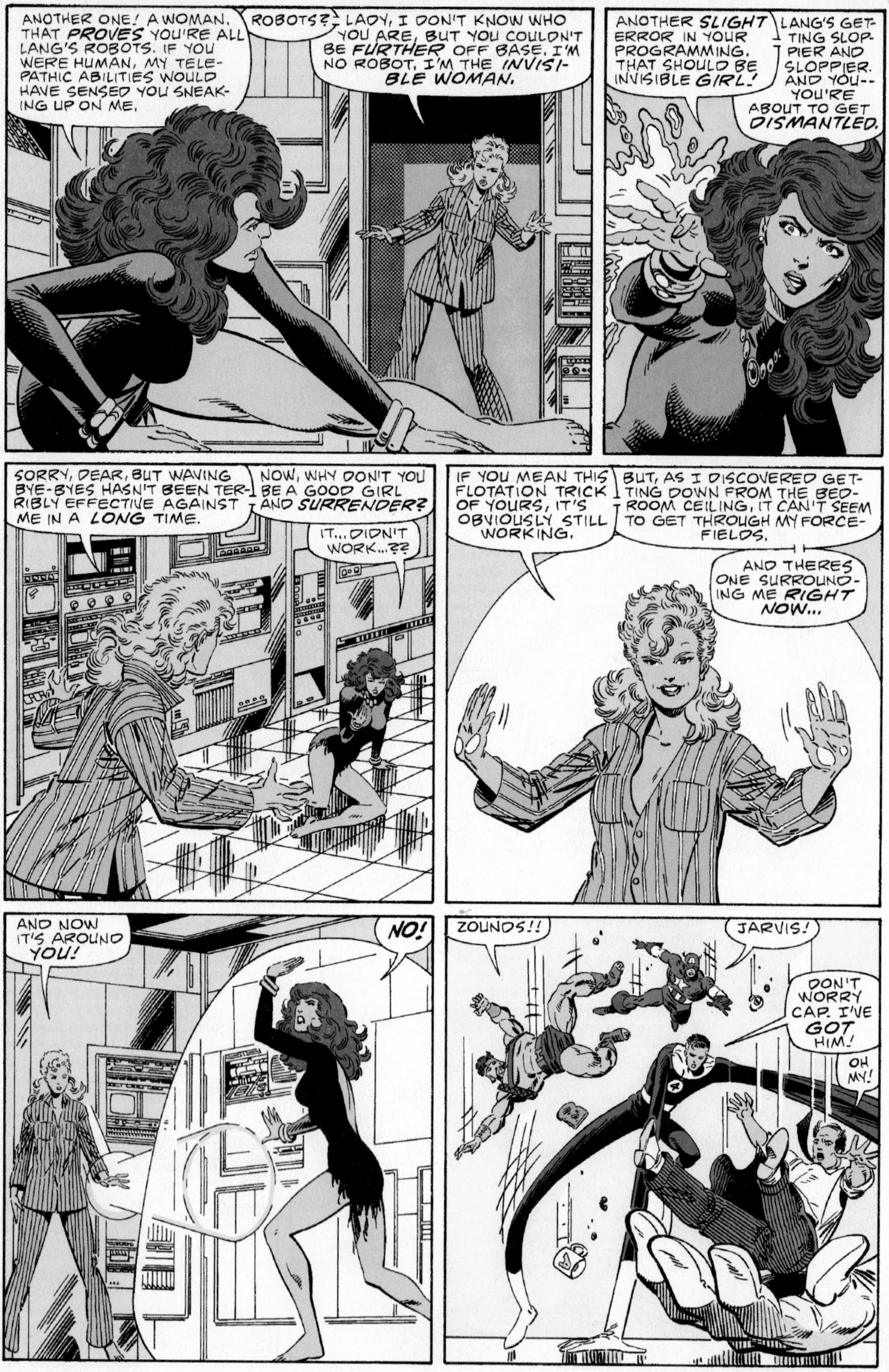
ANOTHER ONE! A WOMAN. THAT PROVES YOU'RE ALL LANG'S ROBOTS. IF YOU WERE HUMAN, MY TELEPATHIC ABILITIES WOULD HAVE SENSED YOU SNEAKING UP ON ME.
ROBOTS?
LADY, I DON'T KNOW WHO YOU ARE, BUT YOU COULDN'T BE FURTHER OFF BASE. I'M NO ROBOT. I'M THE INVISIBLE WOMAN.
ANOTHER SLIGHT ERROR IN YOUR PROGRAMMING. THAT SHOULD BE INVISIBLE GIRL!
LANG'S GETTING SLOPPIER AND SLOPPIER. AND YOU--YOU'RE ABOUT TO GET DISMANTLED.
SORRY, DEAR, BUT WAVING BYE-BYES HASN'T BEEN TERRIBLY EFFECTIVE AGAINST ME IN A LONG TIME.
NOW, WHY DON'T YOU BE A GOOD GIRL AND SURRENDER?
IT... DIDN'T WORK...??
IF YOU MEAN THIS FLOTATION TRICK OF YOURS, IT'S OBVIOUSLY STILL WORKING.
BUT, AS I DISCOVERED GETTING DOWN FROM THE BEDROOM CEILING, IT CAN'T SEEM TO GET THROUGH MY FORCEFIELDS.
AND THERES ONE SURROUNDING ME RIGHT NOW...
AND NOW IT'S AROUND YOU!
NO!
ZOUNDS!!
JARVIS!
DON'T WORRY CAP. I'VE GOT HIM!
OH MY!

OKAY, CREEPS. YOU'VE **WON.**

GET IT OVER WITH.

KILL ME.

BOY, I'VE SEEN **PERSECUTION COMPLEXES** IN MY DAY, BUT THIS LADY TAKES THE CAKE!

AND PERHAPS NOT WITHOUT **JUSTIFICATION,** SUE. A MOMENT WHILE I TURN OFF THE BIO-STIMULATOR...

NOW, LET'S SEE IF MY **HUNCH** IS CORRECT AS TO WHO OUR GUEST REALLY IS...

OF **COURSE.**

YOU'RE **MARVEL GIRL,** ARE YOU NOT?

WHY DO YOU INSIST ON CONTINUING THIS STUPID CHARADE?

WHAT DOES LANG HOPE TO GAIN FROM IT ALL?

DOES HE EXPECT ME TO **GROVEL?** TO BEG FOR MY LIFE?

WE'RE MADE OF **TOUGHER** STUFF THAN **THAT** IN THE X-MEN!

X-MEN? MARVEL GIRL? OF COURSE! BUT NO ONE'S SEEN OR HEARD ANYTHING OF **HER** IN... **YEARS!**

NOT SINCE SEVERAL **CHRISTMAS EVES** PAST.

AND THAT VERY PROBABLY ACCOUNTS, IN PART, FOR HER **HOSTILITY.**

SUE, **DROP YOUR FIELD!**

ART THOU MAD? IF SHE DOTH ATTACK AGAIN...

SHE **WON'T.** NOT IF WE **CONVINCE** HER THAT WE TRULY ARE WHO WE SAY WE ARE...

...BY PLACING OURSELVES **COMPLETELY** AT HER MERCY!

I...I DON'T UNDER-STAND...

IF YOU'RE **REALLY** THE FANTASTIC FOUR ...**REALLY** THE AVENGERS...

THEN...WHAT'S **HAPPENED** TO ME? I FEEL SO...SO **TIRED...**

SO UTTERLY... **DRAINED...**

EASY, MISS, EASY! PERHAPS YOU SHOULD SIT DOWN. AND WOULD YOU CARE FOR SOME NICE HOT *TEA?*

YOU SEEM VERY... CONFUSED.

AND WHO WOULDN'T BE? I HAVE THE AWFUL FEELING A GIGANTIC *HOLE* HAS JUST BEEN PUNCHED THROUGH MY *LIFE.*

THE LAST THING I CLEARLY REMEMBER WAS... *CHRISTMAS EVE...* I WAS HAVING DINNER AT ROCKEFELLER PLAZA WITH... A FRIEND... WHEN...

IT CAN'T BE THEM!

NOT THEM!

PREPARE TO FACE YOUR DOOM, MUTANT, FOR--

THE SENTINELS HAVE RETURNED!

"WE'D BATTLED THOSE MUTANT-HUNTING ROBOTS BEFORE, BUT THIS TIME IT WAS *DIFFERENT.* THIS TIME THEY SEEMED TO BE PART OF A *GOVERNMENT-APPROVED* OPERATION, LEAD BY A MADMAN NAMED *STEPHEN LANG...*"

"LANG'S BASE WAS ABOARD S.H.I.E.L.D.'S GIANT ORBITAL PLATFORM. THE REST OF THE X-MEN VIRTUALLY *HI-JACKED* A NASA SHUTTLE TO ATTEMPT A RESCUE OF THOSE OF US WHO HAD BEEN CAPTURED."

MUTANT-KIND ARE THE ENEMY. I'M TO FIND A WAY TO *DESTROY YOU!*

"THAT WAS WHEN LANG UNLEASHED HIS MOST HEINOUS PLOY...

"HIS X-*SENTINELS!*

"*ERSATZ* VERSIONS OF ICEMAN, BEAST, ANGEL, CYCLOPS, PROFESSOR X--YES, AND EVEN *ME!*

"SET TO FIGHT WOLVERINE, NIGHTCRAWLER, BANSHEE, STORM, AND *COLOSSUS.*

"THEY BATTLED THE NEW X-MEN ALMOST TO A STAND-STILL..."

"THEN, AT THE LAST POSSIBLE MOMENT BEFORE COMPLETE DEFEAT, THE TIDE WAS SUDDENLY, IRREVOCABLY TURNED.

"WOLVERINE, WHO SEEMS TO POSSESS SENSES HONED BEYOND ANY HUMAN LEVELS, GUESSED THE TRUE NATURE OF THE ATTACKERS.

"AND IN ONE TERRIBLE, BLINDING SLASH OF HIS INDESTRUCTABLE CLAWS, THAT NATURE LAY REVEALED."

LANG'S SCHEME FELL APART, LIKE THE FRAGILE HOUSE OF CARDS IT TRULY WAS.

ONCE AGAIN THE X-MEN HAD TRIUMPHED OVER THE FORCES OF BIGOTRY AND PREJUDICE, FORCES THAT SOUGHT TO STAMP OUT THOSE OF US WHO ARE *MUTANTS,* BORN WITH SPECIAL *EXTRA* POWERS...

...SOUGHT TO OBLITERATE US FOR NO MORE REASON THAN THAT WE ARE *DIFFERENT.*

AND THEN... AND THEN... I *KNOW* SOMETHING ELSE HAPPENED AFTER WE BEAT LANG AND HIS SENTINELS. SOMETHING *HORRIBLE.*

SOMETHING THAT BURST ANY SENSE OF VICTORY WE MIGHT HAVE FELT. POPPED IT LIKE A SOAP BUBBLE.

BUT... I CAN'T REMEMBER WHAT IT WAS... I JUST CAN'T REMEMBER.

THAT STORY HAS A POWERFUL RING OF *TRUTH.* I REMEMBER WELL THE REAPPEARANCE OF THE SENTINELS ON THAT PARTICULAR CHRISTMAS EVE.

YES. AND I RECALL THE GOVERNMENT DISAVOWING KNOWLEDGE OR SUPPORT OF LANG'S *"FINAL SOLUTION."*

BUT, REED, NONE OF THIS EXPLAINS HOW THIS POOR GIRL WOUND UP IN THAT *POD* AT THE BOTTOM OF JAMAICA BAY!

HOW CAN WE GET INTO THE *CLOSED* PART OF HER MEMORY? COULD YOU USE THE BIO-STIMULATOR AGAIN?

NO.

NO, SUE. WE DARE NOT USE IT ON HER AGAIN. I WOULD NEVER HAVE USED IT IN THE FIRST PLACE, HAD I KNOWN WE WERE DEALING WITH AN *ESPER.**

AS IT IS, IT'S A *MIRACLE* SHE DID NOT SUFFER PERMANENT *BRAIN DAMAGE.* A SECOND EXPOSURE WOULD ALMOST CERTAINLY CAUSE IRREPARABLE HARM!

I WILL NOT RISK THAT!

* SOMEONE WITH HIGHLY DEVELOPED *MENTAL POWERS.*

BUT...THERE MUST BE SOMETHING TO BE DONE, MASTER REED. SOME WAY OF ASSISTING THIS UNFORTUNATE WAIF.

IF THERE IS, JARVIS, I'M AFRAID I CAN'T IMAGINE WHAT IT IS...

I CAN!

PROFESSOR X, THE LEADER OF THE X-MEN! HE POSSESSES THE MOST POWERFUL TELEPATHIC MIND ON EARTH!

HE SHOULD BE ABLE TO PROBE THROUGH THIS FOG IN MY HEAD, AND SEE WHAT HAPPENED!

I HAVE TO GET BACK TO THE X-MEN!

JUST A MOMENT, MISS. I'D SAY THAT THAT'S NOT THE BEST OF IDEAS, CONSIDERING THEY'RE ASSOCIATING WITH A KNOWN CRIMINAL!

WHAT?!? WHAT ARE YOU TALKING ABOUT? PROFESSOR X WOULD NEVER...

BUT IT'S TRUE, MARVEL GIRL.

WE HAVE SEEN THE X-MEN FIGHTING SIDE-BY-SIDE WITH THE MUTANT KNOWN AS MAGNETO!

WH-AAATTT?

THAT CAN'T BE! IT CAN'T!!!

UNLESS THEY'VE BEEN BRAIN WASHED...

I WISH IT WERE THAT SIMPLE, MARVEL GIRL...WE HAVE SEEN THE X-MEN WITH MAGNETO...*

...AND WHATEVER THEY'RE DOING THEY SEEM TO BE DOING IT VOLUNTARILY!

THIS...THIS CAN'T BE HAPPENING! I DON'T KNOW WHERE I AM, WHEN I AM...

PLEASE, THERE'S ONLY ONE OTHER PLACE I CAN GO, ONE OTHER PLACE I CAN KEEP FROM LOSING MY MIND!

MY PARENTS' HOUSE.

PLEASE... PLEASE HELP ME TO GET HOME...

OF COURSE. OF COURSE WE WILL.

WE MUST!

*IN THE FIRST SECRET WARS LIMITED SERIES.

46

I'M AFRAID THAT SCENARIO IS NO MORE ACCEPTABLE THAN THE FIRST, SUE.

REED? WHY NOT?

YES, WHY NOT... SURELY THAT'S THE *SAFEST* PLACE FOR ME! UNLESS YOU KNOW SOMETHING ABOUT MY PARENTS!

NOT AT ALL, MARVEL GIRL. I KNOW NOTHING AT ALL ABOUT YOUR PARENTS.

...EXCEPT THAT THEY HAVE MOST LIKELY BE- LIEVED YOU TO BE *DEAD* FOR SEVERAL YEARS NOW...

...AND THE SUDDEN SHOCK OF SEEING YOU AGAIN MIGHT--

OH, NO! IT JUST WON'T *STOP*!!

VERILY, THOU ART SURELY *RIGHT*, REED RICHARDS, AND MERE MORTALS, SUCH AS THEY MUST BE, WOULD SCARCE BE ABLE TO ACCEPT THEIR CHILD'S RETURN FROM *PLU- TO'S* DARK REALM!

A LITTLE ON THE *PO- ETIC* SIDE, BUT AN AC- CURATE ASSESSMENT, HERCULES.

THERE ARE SO MANY FACTORS TO BE CONSIDERED HERE, BEFORE WE CAN *ACT.*

NO!

I DON'T MAKE A HABIT OF DISAGREEING WITH YOU, DARLING, BUT I'M *CALLING YOU* ON THIS ONE. MARVEL GIRL'S ON THE VERGE OF A *NERVOUS BREAKDOWN.*

SHE NEEDS FAMILIAR SURROUNDINGS, THINGS SHE CAN HOOK INTO TO KEEP HER FROM SAILING OVER THE *EDGE.*

...please... please...

BUT, SUE...

NO "BUTS," REED. I HAVE A PRETTY CLEAR IDEA OF WHAT SHE'S GO- ING THROUGH.

I'VE JUST BARELY STARTED RECOVERING, MYSELF, FROM THE MENTAL TURMOIL THE *PSYCHO-MAN* PUT ME THROUGH.* BELIEVE ME WHEN I SAY I KNOW WHAT MARVEL GIRL *NEEDS.*

...please...

*IN ISSUE #S 280 THROUGH 282.

...VERY WELL. I DO NOT CARE FOR THIS PLAN, BUT... WE'LL TAKE HER TO HER PARENT'S HOUSE.

THE SON OF ZEUS HAS NE'ER DESERTED A MAIDEN IN *DISTRESS*, FRIEND REED!

NOR HAVE I... BUT I'LL HAVE TO CATCH UP WITH YOU *LATER*, IF I CAN. THERE'S... SOMETHING I WANT TO CHECK OUT, FIRST.

COMING, CAP? HERCULES?

THERE IT IS--ANNANDALE ROAD. LUCKILY YOUR PARENT'S HOUSE IS FAIRLY *ISOLATED.*

WE WON'T DISTRESS TOO MANY NEIGHBORS LANDING HERE.

STILL ONLY GETTING THEIR TELEPHONE ANSWERING MACHINE, REED.

Hm! I WAS *HOPING* THEY'D BE HOME BY NOW, MARVEL GIRL, I DON'T SUPPOSE YOU HAVE ANY IDEA WHERE THEY MIGHT BE?

NOT A CLUE, SORRY. AND ...I GUESS IT'S TIME YOU STARTED CALLING ME *JEAN,* MY NAME IS *JEAN GREY.*

A *HUMBLE* EDIFICE, YET I SUPPOSE TO ONE NOT RAISED 'PON THE SLOPES OF *OLYMPUS,* 'TWOULD BE *PLEASANT* ENOUGH.

THIS PORTAL APPEARS TO BE *LOCKED.*

NO MATTER!

KRAK!

HERCULES!! WHAT DO YOU THINK YOU'RE *DOING?!?*

THIS ISN'T THE FORTRESS HIDE-OUT OF SOME WOULD-BE WORLD-BEATER!

THIS IS MY PARENTS' *HOME!*

A THOUSAND PARDONS, LADY JEAN. I DID *MISJUDGE* THE STRENGTH OF THE DOOR.

'TWAS MY INTENT TO FORCE THE *LOCK...*

BUT YOU DIDN'T EVEN NEED TO DO *THAT!* LOOK, UNDER THIS FAKE ROCK IN THE BORDER...

DON'T WORRY, JEAN. WE'LL REPLACE THE DOOR.

THE SPARE KEY!

SHALL WE GO *INSIDE* NOW?

YES...) BUT...IT'S ALL SO *STRANGE.* IT'S ONLY A FEW *WEEKS* FOR ME SINCE I WAS LAST HERE, BUT FOR THE REST OF THE WORLD...

ZOUNDS!!

48

WHAT *IS* IT, HERCULES?

THIS... ICON, FRIEND REED. I DIOST BETAKE IT FOR A SIMPLE *REPRESENTATION* OF THE FAIR JEAN. BUT 'TIS *MORE*! 'TIS MUCH, *MUCH* MORE!

FASCINATING!! THIS CAN ONLY BE A *HOLEMPATHIC MATRIX CRYSTAL*! SUCH THINGS ARE THEORETICALLY POSSIBLE, BUT MANY *THOUSANDS* OF YEARS BEYOND CURRENT *EARTH* TECHNOLOGY.

'TIS A REMARKABLE DEVICE, IF DEVICE IT BE. AN EXPERIENCE OF... OF NIGH *EMBARRASSING* INTIMACY!

"EMBARRASSING...?" REED, WHAT IN THE WORLD IS THAT THING?

WELL, SUE, "EMBARRASSING" IS ONLY HERCULES' EVALUATION IT'S A MEANS OF RECORDING THE VERY *ESSENCE* OF A LIVING BEING, SUE, THEIR *THOUGHTS*, THEIR *DREAMS*. TO TOUCH IT IS TO EXPERIENCE EVERYTHING THAT MADE THE SUBJECT *WHO* AND *WHAT* THEY HAD BEEN IN *LIFE*!

AND... AND THIS... CRYSTAL... IT'S... *ME*?!? HOW COULD *MY PARENTS* HAVE COME TO OWN SUCH A THING?

THAT I CANNOT BEGIN TO GUESS, MISS GREY.

BUT IT *IS* AN ANSWER TO OUR PROBLEM! IN THEORY, SUCH AN OBJECT WOULD NEVER COME INTO CONTACT WITH THE PERSONALITY IT RECORDS. IT IS, AFTER ALL, A *MEMORIUM*, AN *ELEGY* TO THE DEPARTED.

BUT IF *YOU* WERE TO HOLD THIS, MISS GREY, IF *YOU* WERE TO EXPERIENCE WHAT LIES LOCKED WITHIN IT...

BUT... BUT FOR SUCH A THING TO EXIST... IT MUST HAVE BEEN MADE AFTER I... AFTER I...

...DIED...

YES, AND WITH *LUCK* IT WILL CONTAIN AN IMPRESSION OF THE MISSING MOMENTS OF YOUR MEMORY.

TAKE IT, MISS GREY.

NO! I... I *CAN'T*! I... KNOW THIS IS WHAT WE CAME HERE FOR, I KNOW IT'S THE *ANSWER*, BUT...

...BUT I'M *AFRAID*!

MASTER CAP, YOU SEEM MOST... RESTIVE.

DO I, JARVIS? AND HERE I THOUGHT I WAS WEARING MY BEST *POKER FACE.*

IT'S THIS *MARVEL GIRL* BUSINESS.

I'VE BEEN RE-CHECKING ALL OUR *DATA* ON HER. *SOMETHING* KEEPS PINGING AWAY AT MY OLD *BATTLE-SENSE.*

SHE SEEMED *HARMLESS* ENOUGH, ONCE SHE CALMED DOWN. HAVE YOU *CROSS-REFERENCED* HER FILE WITH ANYONE ELSE'S?

NO. BUT I THINK THAT *MAY* BE WHAT'S BOTHERING ME.

IT'S THE *X-MEN* CONNECTION. I KEEP AS-SOCIATING HER WITH...

THE BEAST! OF COURSE!!

AVENGERS SECURITY REFER-ENCE FILE OMEGA SEVEN DELTA. THE *BEAST* RECORDING. SUBJECT: JEAN GREY, A.K.A. *MARVEL GIRL.*

JEAN AND I*, ALONG WITH CYCLOPS, ICEMAN, AND ANGEL, WERE THE *FOUNDING MEMBERS* OF THE ORIGINAL X-MEN TEAM.

*THE BEAST SHOWN HERE BE-FORE HE MUTATED FULLY TO HIS FURRED STATE.

JEAN IS *DEAD* NOW. BUT BE-FORE SHE DIED, SOME-THING HAPPENED TO HER. ON A SPACE-SHUTTLE RETURNING TO EARTH, SHE WAS EXPOSED TO A MASSIVE DOSE OF *COS-MIC RADIATION.*

SHE EMERGED FROM THE CRASH *TRANSFORMED.* SHE HAD BECOME INFINITELY *POWERFUL* AND CALLED HER-SELF THE *PHOENIX.*

SOMETHING IN THAT TERRIBLE POWER *CORRUPTED* JEAN. SHE SEEMINGLY BECAME *TOTALLY EVIL.* SHE THREATENED TO *DESTROY THE WORLD,* PERHAPS THE *UNIVERSE ITSELF!*

THEN, SOMEHOW SHE RE-GAINED CONTROL OF HERSELF, AND IN A DARK, LOST CAVERN ON THE *MOON,* USED AN ANCIENT ALIEN WEAPON, BUR-IED FOR MILLENNIA IN THE LUNAR DUST-- USED IT TO DESTROY *HERSELF,* AND SAVE US ALL!

JEAN GREY IS *GONE*, ONLY A *HOLEMPATHIC CRYSTAL*, A GIFT FROM THE ALIEN *SH'IAR*, REMAINS TO COMMEMORATE HER. AND THE AWESOME POWER OF THE PHOENIX IS DISPERSED BACK INTO THE COSMIC *VOID* FROM WHENCE IT CAME, OR SO I *PRAY.*

FOR WE, HUMANITY, *LIFE-KIND,* WERE *VERY, VERY LUCKY* THIS TIME. AND IF THE AWFUL POWER OF THE PHOENIX SHOULD EVER SOMEHOW *REAPPEAR,* THEN IT COULD SIGNAL THE END OF *EVERYTHING!*

HEAVEN HELP US ALL!!

...OH... MY...!

I CAN APPRECIATE YOUR *CONFLICT,* JEAN. BUT THIS IS YOUR ONLY HOPE, THE ONLY *KEY* TO YOUR PRISON.

AND IF IT CONTAINS THE MEMORY OF MY *DEATH?*

IF IT SOMEHOW SHOWS ME I'M *NOT* JEAN GREY? THAT I'M A *GHOST,* THAT I'M... I'M...

IF YOU WERE *TRULY* ONE OF THE FIRST X-MEN, JEAN, THEN YOU HAVE FACED GREATER TERRORS IN THE PAST.

WHATEVER *STRENGTH* GUIDED YOU THEN, SUMMON IT NOW, YOU *MUST* FACE WHATEVER THE CRYSTAL HOLDS.

V-VERY WELL, PROFESSOR RICHARDS. IT'S TRUE, IN MY TIME I'VE WALKED INTO THE VERY JAWS OF *HADES.*

WHAT CAN THIS LITTLE PIECE OF *GLASS* HOLD THAT COULD POSSIBLY BE WORSE THAN *THAT?*

BEARD OF MY FATHER! WHAT DOTH TRANSPIRE?

THE CRYSTAL! ITS POWER SOURCE HAS TEMPORARILY REVITALIZED HER FAILING TELEPATHIC POWERS!

WE'RE *SEEING* WHAT SHE'S *REMEMBERING!*

THESE MUST BE THE EVENTS BLANKED OUT BY THE TRAUMA OF...

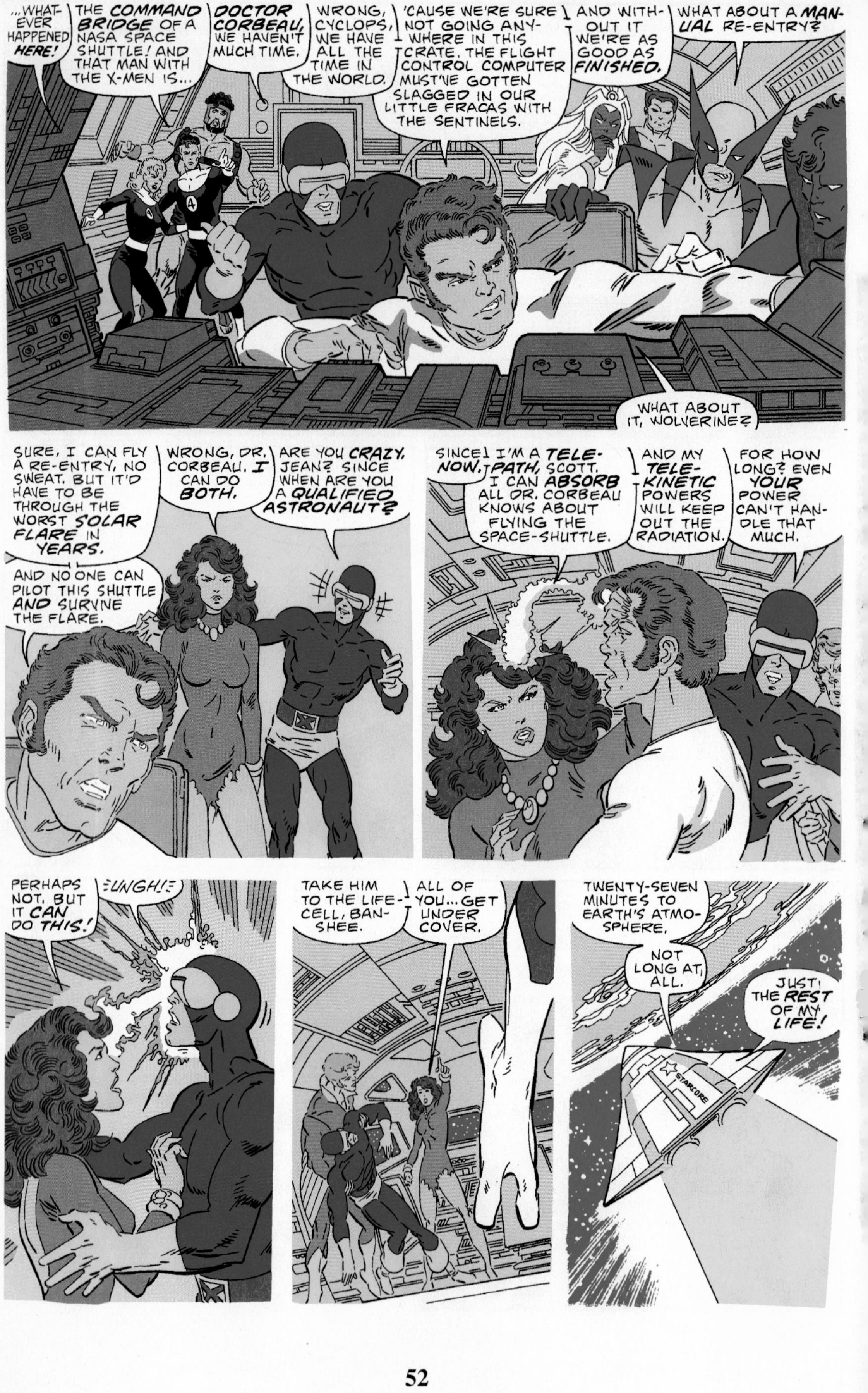
...WHAT-EVER HAPPENED HERE!
THE COMMAND BRIDGE OF A NASA SPACE SHUTTLE! AND THAT MAN WITH THE X-MEN IS...
DOCTOR CORBEAU, WE HAVEN'T MUCH TIME.
WRONG, CYCLOPS, WE HAVE ALL THE TIME IN THE WORLD.
'CAUSE WE'RE SURE NOT GOING ANYWHERE IN THIS CRATE. THE FLIGHT CONTROL COMPUTER MUST'VE GOTTEN SLAGGED IN OUR LITTLE FRACAS WITH THE SENTINELS.
AND WITHOUT IT WE'RE AS GOOD AS FINISHED.
WHAT ABOUT A MANUAL RE-ENTRY?
WHAT ABOUT IT, WOLVERINE?
SURE, I CAN FLY A RE-ENTRY, NO SWEAT. BUT IT'D HAVE TO BE THROUGH THE WORST SOLAR FLARE IN YEARS.
AND NO ONE CAN PILOT THIS SHUTTLE AND SURVIVE THE FLARE.
WRONG, DR. CORBEAU. I CAN DO BOTH.
ARE YOU CRAZY, JEAN? SINCE WHEN ARE YOU A QUALIFIED ASTRONAUT?
SINCE NOW.
I'M A TELEPATH, SCOTT. I CAN ABSORB ALL DR. CORBEAU KNOWS ABOUT FLYING THE SPACE-SHUTTLE.
AND MY TELEKINETIC POWERS WILL KEEP OUT THE RADIATION.
FOR HOW LONG? EVEN YOUR POWER CAN'T HANDLE THAT MUCH.
PERHAPS NOT. BUT IT CAN DO THIS!
UNGH!
TAKE HIM TO THE LIFE-CELL, BANSHEE.
ALL OF YOU... GET UNDER COVER.
TWENTY-SEVEN MINUTES TO EARTH'S ATMOSPHERE.
NOT LONG AT ALL.
JUST THE REST OF MY LIFE!
STARCORE

Panel 1:

TACTACTACTACTACT

REED... THAT SOUND...

COSMIC RAY BOM-BARD-MENT!

JUST LIKE THE ONE THAT GAVE US OUR POWERS!

MY SCREEN'S GIVING WAY!

THE FLARE-- THE RADIA-TION-- IT'S STARTING TO GET *THROUGH!*

SCOTT!

Panel 2:

SHE'S *DYING,* REED-- BEFORE OUR EYES!

THIS COULD HAVE BEEN *OUR* FATE, HAD THE RAYS NOT TRANSFORMED US INTO THE *FANTAS-TIC FOUR!*

IT'S TOO *HORRIBLE--* REED, MAKE JEAN STOP! SHE DOESN'T DESERVE TO ENDURE SUCH HORROR A SECOND TIME!

Panel 3:

YET-- MY FRIENDS-- FOR ALL HER PAIN-- SHE DOTH NOT YIELD.

'TIS COURAGE THAT WOULD DO THE NOBLEST OLYMPIAN PROUD!

I'VE COME THIS FAR, MRS. RICHARDS. I'LL SEE IT THROUGH TO THE END. I HAVE TO.

Panel 4:

BUT HOW COULD I-- HOW COULD *ANYONE--* HAVE SURVIVED-- ≷GASP!?!≷

ALL OF YOU-- *LOOK!*

WHAT...?!?

I'M HALLUCIN-ATING-- MY MIND'S GOING -- I SEE A LIGHT, I HEAR ...*MUSIC?!* THIS IS *INSANE!*

Panel 5:

MY PAIN-- I DON'T FEEL IT ANYMORE!

NO! NO!!

I CAN'T BE DYING-- NOT YET, IT'S *TOO SOON--* TOO MUCH DEPENDS ON ME!

I *WON'T* FAIL MY FRIENDS -- MY *LOVE!*

Panel 6:

DON'T BE AFRAID.

I MEAN NO HARM.

WHO-- WHAT-- *ARE* YOU?!

I'LL SECOND THAT QUESTION.

REED, ANY IDEAS--?!

THE SHUTTLE HAS EVIDENTLY BEEN INFILTRATED BY A FORCE-- OR ENTITY-- COMPOSED OF PURE ENERGY.

BUT...WHY HATH THE WORLD GROWN STILL ABOUT US?

TIME WARP!

THAT ENTITY HAS FROZEN TIME AROUND US WHILE IT DOES... WHAT IT'S DOING.

BUT... WHAT IS IT DOING ???

I AM FIRE.

A FORCE OF LIFE.

YOU CALLED OUT FOR AID. I ANSWERED.

YOUR FORM IS SO FRAGILE-- HOW CAN YOU POSSIBLY ENDURE?

PLEASE--DON'T... CONCERN YOURSELF WITH ME--I'M ALREADY DEAD. I'M JUST... TOO DARN STUBBORN TO QUIT.

BUT, IF YOU CAN--SAVE THE X-MEN!

ESPECIALLY... SCOTT?

HOW DO YOU KNOW?!

MY CONSCIOUSNESS --MY FORM, AND IT'S ABILITY TO COMMUNI- CATE ON THIS PLANE OF EXISTENCE--DERIVE FROM YOU. THEY PROVIDE AN... AWARENESS OF YOUR DOMINANT EMOTIONS AND MEMORIES.

OH, GREAT-- YOU MEAN YOU'RE A FIGMENT OF MY IMAGIN- ATION?

IN PART.

YOU ARE HUMAN, JEAN GREY. I AM OF THE UNIVERSE.

54

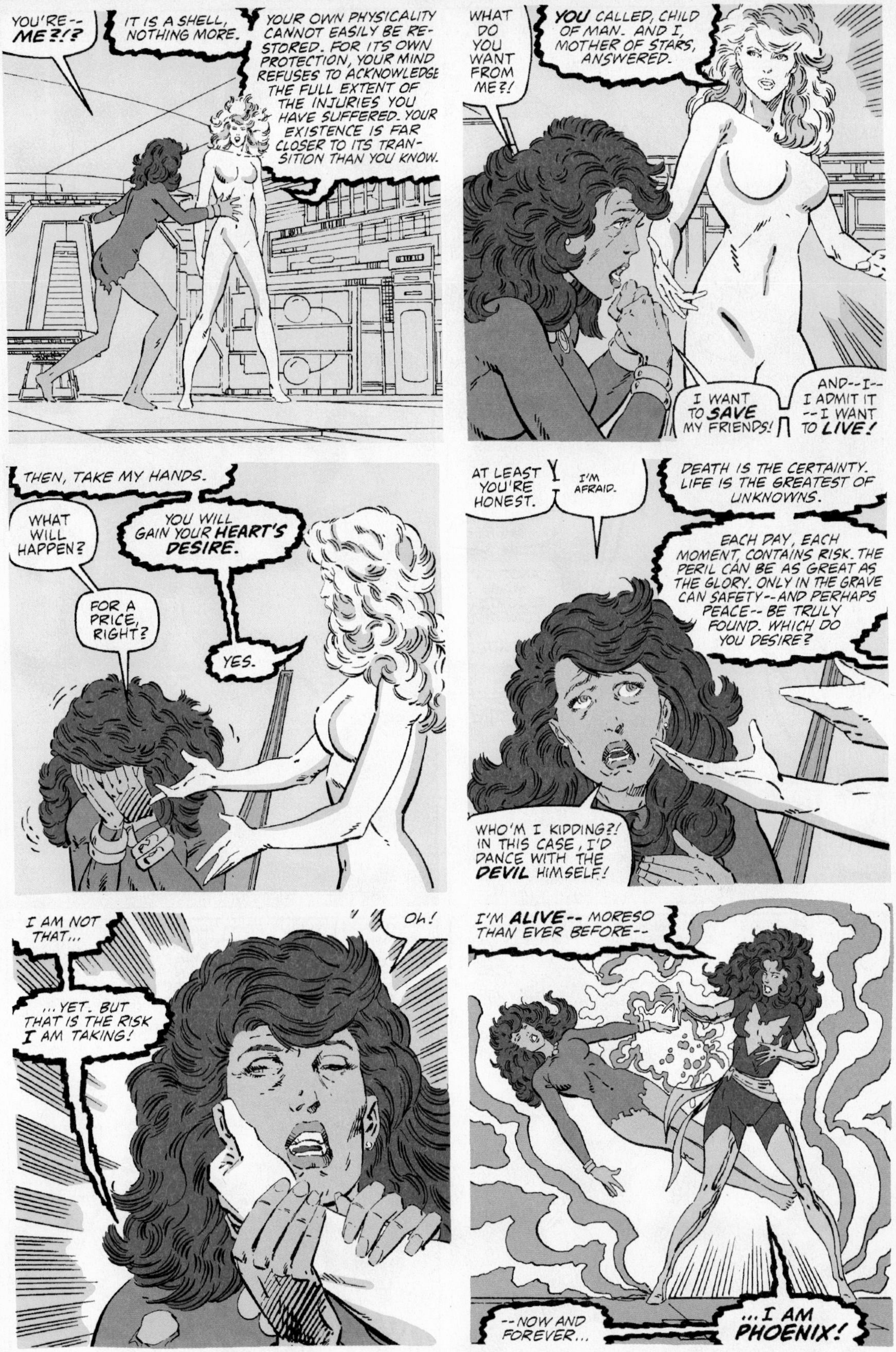
YOU'RE-- ME?!?
IT IS A SHELL, NOTHING MORE.
YOUR OWN PHYSICALITY CANNOT EASILY BE RESTORED. FOR ITS OWN PROTECTION, YOUR MIND REFUSES TO ACKNOWLEDGE THE FULL EXTENT OF THE INJURIES YOU HAVE SUFFERED. YOUR EXISTENCE IS FAR CLOSER TO ITS TRANSITION THAN YOU KNOW.
WHAT DO YOU WANT FROM ME?!
YOU CALLED, CHILD OF MAN. AND I, MOTHER OF STARS, ANSWERED.
I WANT TO SAVE MY FRIENDS!
AND--I-- I ADMIT IT --I WANT TO LIVE!
THEN, TAKE MY HANDS.
WHAT WILL HAPPEN?
YOU WILL GAIN YOUR HEART'S DESIRE.
FOR A PRICE, RIGHT?
YES.
AT LEAST YOU'RE HONEST.
I'M AFRAID.
DEATH IS THE CERTAINTY. LIFE IS THE GREATEST OF UNKNOWNS.
EACH DAY, EACH MOMENT, CONTAINS RISK. THE PERIL CAN BE AS GREAT AS THE GLORY. ONLY IN THE GRAVE CAN SAFETY--AND PERHAPS PEACE--BE TRULY FOUND. WHICH DO YOU DESIRE?
WHO'M I KIDDING?! IN THIS CASE, I'D DANCE WITH THE DEVIL HIMSELF!
I AM NOT THAT...
...YET. BUT THAT IS THE RISK I AM TAKING!
Oh!
I'M ALIVE-- MORESO THAN EVER BEFORE--
--NOW AND FOREVER...
...I AM PHOENIX!

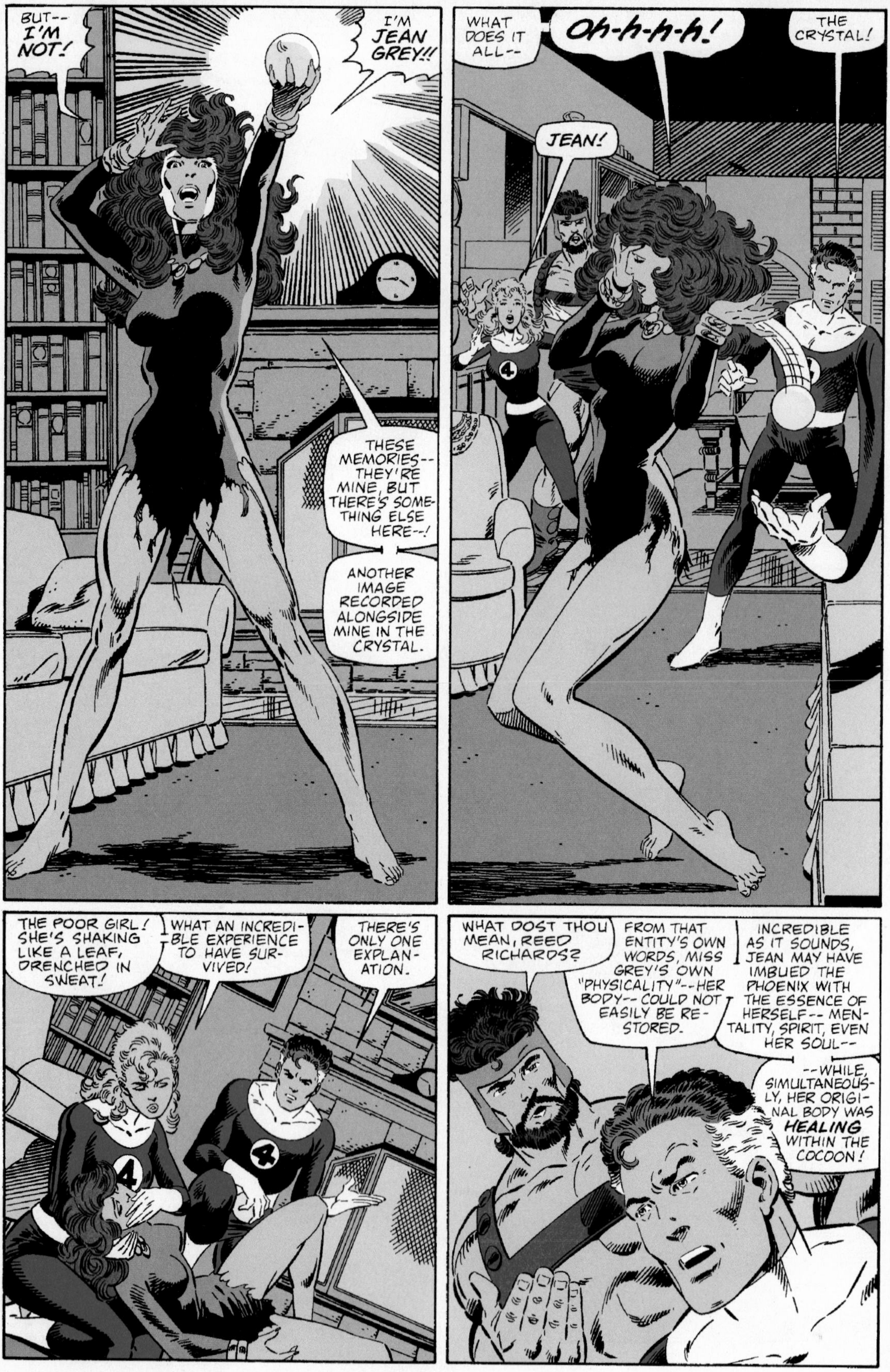

BUT-- I'M NOT!
I'M JEAN GREY!!
THESE MEMORIES-- THEY'RE MINE, BUT THERE'S SOMETHING ELSE HERE--!
ANOTHER IMAGE RECORDED ALONGSIDE MINE IN THE CRYSTAL.
WHAT DOES IT ALL--
Oh-h-h-h!
THE CRYSTAL!
JEAN!
THE POOR GIRL! SHE'S SHAKING LIKE A LEAF, DRENCHED IN SWEAT!
WHAT AN INCREDIBLE EXPERIENCE TO HAVE SURVIVED!
THERE'S ONLY ONE EXPLANATION.
WHAT DOST THOU MEAN, REED RICHARDS?
FROM THAT ENTITY'S OWN WORDS, MISS GREY'S OWN "PHYSICALITY"--HER BODY-- COULD NOT EASILY BE RESTORED.
INCREDIBLE AS IT SOUNDS, JEAN MAY HAVE IMBUED THE PHOENIX WITH THE ESSENCE OF HERSELF-- MENTALITY, SPIRIT, EVEN HER SOUL--
--WHILE, SIMULTANEOUSLY, HER ORIGINAL BODY WAS HEALING WITHIN THE COCOON!

PART OF ME FEELS FINE! I HAVE... ALL MY OWN MEMORIES. ALL MY OWN...

HOPES? LOVES? YOU SEE THE PROBLEM, DON'T YOU?

THE ENERGY CREATURE FORCED ITSELF TO TOTALLY BELIEVE IT WAS JEAN...IN STRIVING FOR SOME KIND OF AUTHENTICITY, ONE MIGHT ASSUME.

BUT... HOW CAN I EVER KNOW I'M REALLY ME, AND NOT THAT...THAT THING? HOW CAN I EVER KNOW FOR SURE?

I THINK I CAN ANSWER THAT.

I CAUGHT THE LAST FEW SECONDS OF THAT PSYCHIC MOVIOLA AS I WAS LANDING MY JET-CYCLE.

AN UNNERVING EXPERIENCE.

BUT IT MATCHES VERY WELL WITH WHAT I LEARNED FROM THE BEASTS' REPORT IN THE AVENGERS' FILES.

THAT SHUTTLE OF YOURS DID CRASH IN JAMAICA BAY. AND IN WHAT MUST STAND AS A MAJOR MIRACLE, THERE WERE NO FATALITIES.

IN FACT, ONE PERSON SEEMED TO COME OUT OF THE WRECK EVEN BETTER THAN BEFORE.

JEAN GREY.

M...ME?

OR SOMETHING THAT THOUGHT IT WAS YOU. SOMETHING THAT LATER TURNED OUT TO BE THE LIVING EMBODIMENT OF PURE EVIL.

THE CREATURE!

EXACTLY. IT CALLED ITSELF PHOENIX, AND IT WAS WELL ON ITS WAY TO DESTROYING US ALL...

...UNTIL JEAN DEFEATED IT.

ME?!? HOW? I WAS STILL ZONKED OUT ON THE BOTTOM OF THE BAY...

WASN'T I?

Panel 1:

INDEED YOU WERE, JEAN. BUT I CAN SEE CAP'S POINT.

APPARENTLY, THE CREATURE *KNEW* THE RISKS OF TAKING ON A HUMAN FORM... BOTH GOOD AND BAD.

YOU MEAN...

...IT WAS MY HUMANITY THAT TURNED THE FORCE BAD?

Panel 2:

ON THE CONTRARY, MISS GREY... I BELIEVE IT WAS THE POWER OF THE ENTITY *REBELLING AGAINST* THE FORCE OF YOUR WILL THAT TAINTED IT!

THE PHOENIX HAD DUPLICATED YOU DOWN TO THE LAST ATOM OF YOUR STRUCTURE.

IT HAD IMITATED THE PATTERNS OF YOUR BRAIN-WAVES SO PRECISELY THAT EVEN A TRAINED MIND-READER COULD NOT HAVE RECOGNIZED IT FOR WHAT IT WAS.

Panel 3:

YES, YOUR *INNER SELF* COULD NOT BE SUPPRESSED ONCE THE PHOENIX HAD TAKEN IT ON.

YOU GAVE IT YOUR *HUMANITY*, JEAN.

YOU GAVE IT A *SOUL*.

Panel 4:

AND, IN THE LAST MOMENTS, AS IT HOVERED BETWEEN LIGHT AND DARKNESS, UP THERE ON THE MOON, *THAT'S* WHAT MADE THE DIFFERENCE.

BECAUSE THERE'S NO FORCE IN THE UNIVERSE THAT CAN SUPPRESS THE SPLENDOR OF THE HUMAN SPIRIT. AND IT WAS THAT SPIRIT, EVEN IN DUPLICATE FORM, THAT WAS ENOUGH TO DEFEAT THE EVIL POWER OF THE PHOENIX.

EPILOG

WHAT AN *INCREDIBLE* TALE! YOU MUST BE A REMARKABLE YOUNG WOMAN, MISS GREY.

SPARE MY BLUSHES, JARVIS.

I DIDN'T DO ANYTHING ANYONE ELSE WOULDN'T HAVE DONE.

I WOULDN'T BE SO *QUICK* TO PUT MYSELF DOWN IF I WERE YOU, JEAN.

AFTER ALL, IT ISN'T EVERYONE WHO CAN SAVE THE UNIVERSE BY *REMOTE CONTROL!*

MORE LIKE *POST-HYPNOTIC SUGGESTION,* SUE.

AMAZINGLY, THE ONLY SIDE EFFECT TO ALL THAT'S HAPPENED IS THE APPARENT *DAMAGE* TO JEAN'S TELEPATHIC ABILITIES.

HOW DO YOU FEEL TODAY, JEAN?

STILL AT LOOSE ENDS, REED. I'VE DECIDED TO *SAVE* CONTACTING MY FAMILY AND FRIENDS UNTIL I'M BETTER ABLE TO *EXPLAIN* ALL THIS TO THEM.

BUT THAT SORT OF LEAVES ME OUT ON MY LONESOME AGAIN.

PERHAPS. PERHAPS NOT.

I KNOW THAT TWINKLE. WHAT'S ON YOUR MIND?

WELL...IT'S *TRUE* THE X-MEN ARE... "OUT OF BOUNDS." AT LEAST THE *PRESENT* TEAM...

...BUT IT HAS OCCURRED TO ME THERE'S STILL SOMEONE WE CAN CONTACT...

WHO IS REED CALLING? FOR THE AMAZING ANSWER DON'T DARE MISS THE DRAMATIC DEBUT OF MARVEL'S NEWEST SUPER-HIT SENSATION...

X-FACTOR

ON SALE NEXT MONTH! THEN COME BACK TO THE SAME OL' STAND FOR *FANTASTIC FOUR #287* AND A TITANIC TALE TELLINGLY TITLED...

PRISONER OF THE FLESH

FEATURING THE TRIUMPHANT RETURN OF *JOLTIN' JOE SINNOTT!!!*

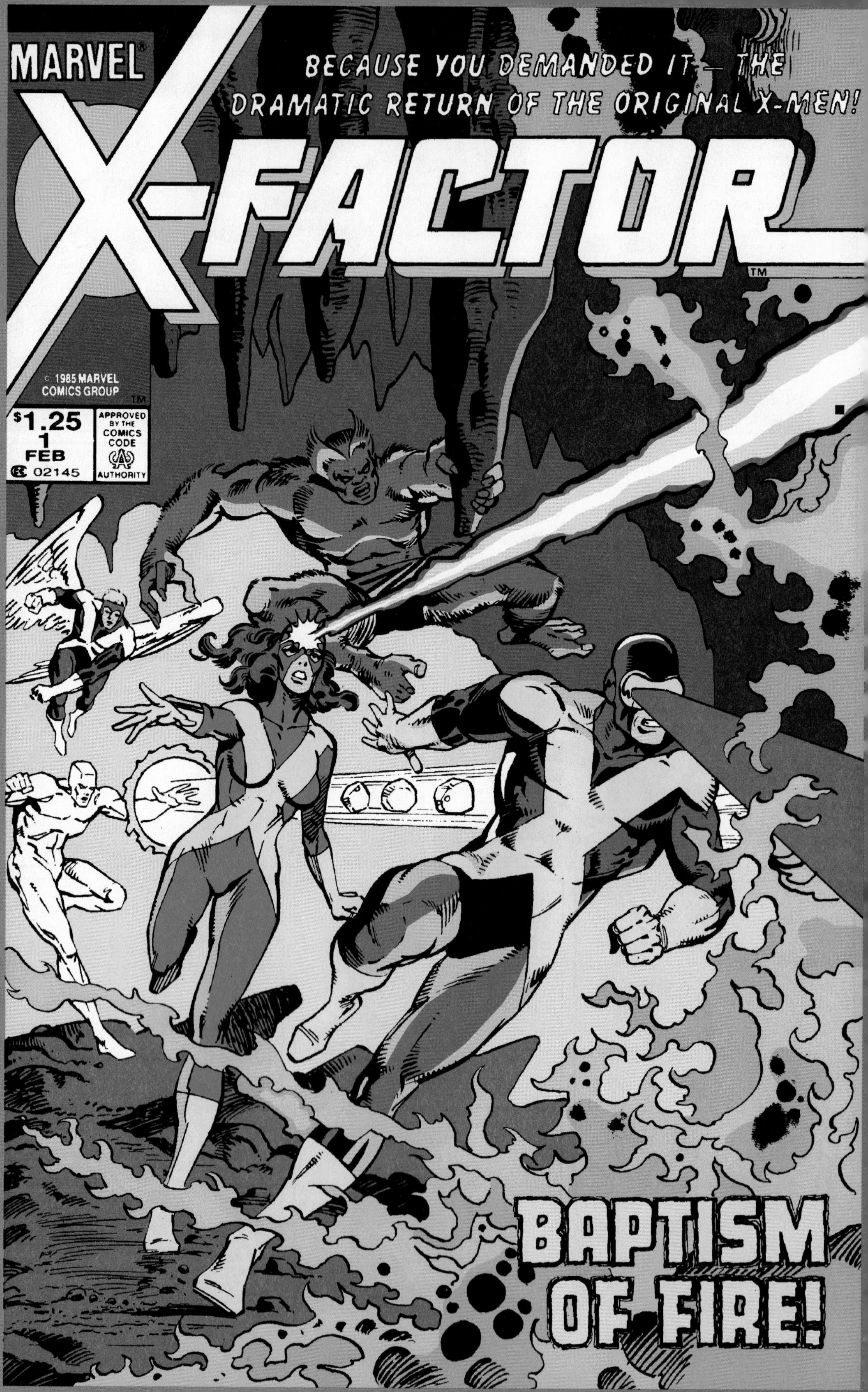
MARVEL®
BECAUSE YOU DEMANDED IT — THE DRAMATIC RETURN OF THE ORIGINAL X-MEN!
X-FACTOR™
© 1985 MARVEL COMICS GROUP
$1.25
1
FEB
02145
APPROVED BY THE COMICS CODE AUTHORITY
BAPTISM OF FIRE!

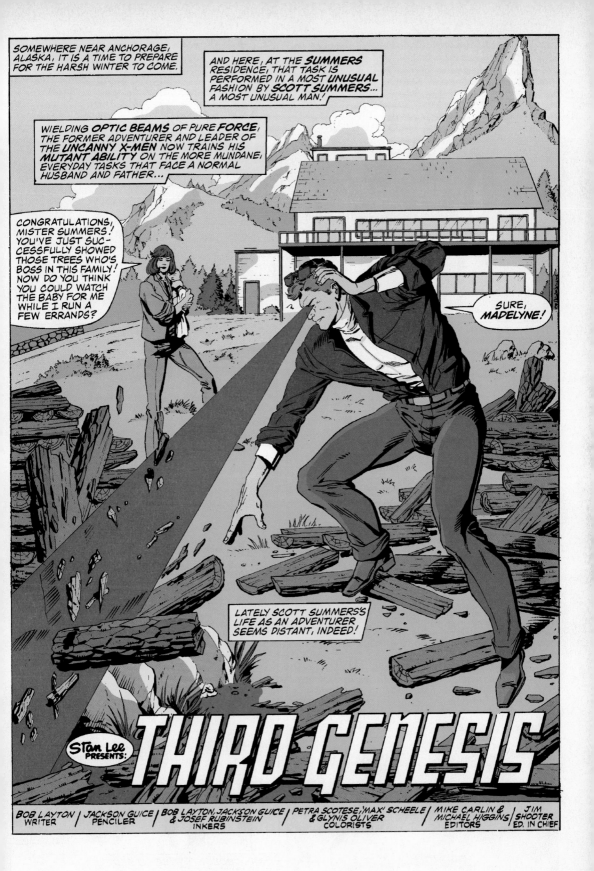

SOMEWHERE NEAR ANCHORAGE, ALASKA, IT IS A TIME TO PREPARE FOR THE HARSH WINTER TO COME.

AND HERE, AT THE *SUMMERS* RESIDENCE, THAT TASK IS PERFORMED IN A MOST *UNUSUAL* FASHION BY *SCOTT SUMMERS*... A MOST UNUSUAL MAN!

WIELDING *OPTIC BEAMS* OF PURE *FORCE*, THE FORMER ADVENTURER AND LEADER OF THE *UNCANNY X-MEN* NOW TRAINS HIS *MUTANT ABILITY* ON THE MORE MUNDANE, EVERYDAY TASKS THAT FACE A NORMAL HUSBAND AND FATHER...

CONGRATULATIONS, MISTER SUMMERS! YOU'VE JUST SUC-CESSFULLY SHOWED THOSE TREES WHO'S BOSS IN THIS FAMILY! NOW DO YOU THINK YOU COULD WATCH THE BABY FOR ME WHILE I RUN A FEW ERRANDS?

SURE, MADELYNE!

LATELY SCOTT SUMMERS'S LIFE AS AN ADVENTURER SEEMS DISTANT, INDEED!

Stan Lee PRESENTS:

THIRD GENESIS

BOB LAYTON / WRITER | JACKSON GUICE / PENCILER | BOB LAYTON, JACKSON GUICE & JOSEF RUBINSTEIN / INKERS | PETRA SCOTESE, 'MAX' SCHEELE & GLYNIS OLIVER / COLORISTS | MIKE CARLIN & MICHAEL HIGGINS / EDITORS | JIM SHOOTER / ED. IN CHIEF

SCOTT, DO WE REALLY NEED ANY MORE WOOD, ANYWAY? YOU'RE ALWAYS OUT IN THE BACK--SPLITTING WOOD! HOUR AFTER HOUR! I DON'T UNDERSTAND YOU! EVEN WHEN YOU'RE HERE, YOU'RE NOT HERE!

OH, NO! THE BABY IS WET! SCOTT, WOULD YOU GRAB ME A DIAPER, PLEASE?

NO PROBLEM.

MEANWHILE, IN OTHER NEWS, THE SENATE COMMITTEE ON MUTANT AFFAIRS IS STILL CONSIDERING LEGISLATION CONCERNING RECENT INCREASES IN HOMO SUPERIOR--OR MUTANT-- ACTIVITY!

MUTANT: MYTH OR MENACE?

PROPOSED LEGIS- LATION WOULD CALL FOR THE MANDATORY REGISTRATION OF ALL KNOWN MUTANTS, MAKING IT NECESSARY FOR THEM TO REPORT THEIR WHEREABOUTS ANNUALLY.

WHAT? THEY CAN'T DO THAT! IT'S GETTING WORSE EVERY DAY, AS IT IS!

NOW, YOU JUST QUIT YOUR SQUIRMING! DADDY'S BRINGING YOU A FRESH DIAPER.

THE MUTANT REGISTRATION BILL COULD POSSIBLY BE ON THE PRESIDENT'S DESK BY EARLY SPRING. IT IS--

SCOTT SUMMERS! I ASKED FOR A LITTLE HELP! IT'S YOUR FELLOW MUTANTS AGAIN, ISN'T IT? HAVEN'T YOU DONE ENOUGH FOR THEM ALREADY? ISN'T IT ABOUT TIME THEY DID SOMETHING FOR THEMSELVES?

IT'S NOT THAT SIMPLE, MADDY.

YOU'RE RIGHT... BUT THINGS AREN'T THAT SIM- PLE HERE EITHER! THINGS HAVE CHANGED, SCOTT. YOU HAVE A RESPONSIBIL- ITY TO YOUR FAMILY NOW! I CAN'T BE THE ONLY ONE WORKING ON THIS MARRIAGE! WE'RE SUPPOSED TO BE IN THIS TOGETHER, AREN'T WE?

DON'T YOU THINK I KNOW THE ONLY REASON YOU CAME BACK TO US AT ALL IS THAT YOU BOMBED OUT IN YOUR BID TO LEAD THE X-MEN? DON'T YOU THINK IT HURTS KNOW- ING THAT? JUST LIKE IT HURTS KNOWING WHY YOU MARRIED ME IN THE FIRST PLACE! BECAUSE I REMINDED YOU OF YOUR OLD FLAME-- THE LATE, BUT NOT FORGOT- TEN JEAN GREY!

MADELYNE! PLEASE, STOP! THAT'S UNCALLED FOR!

NO! I'M TELLING YOU WHAT'S CALLED FOR! I LOVE YOU, SCOTT, AND THE X-MEN DON'T NEED YOU! JEAN IS DEAD! I'M THE ONE THAT NEEDS YOU!

CLICK!

MANY THOUGHTS RACE TO SCOTT SUMMERS'S MIND, BUT HE OFFERS NONE IN HIS DEFENSE.

LATER THAT NIGHT, MADELYNE STIRS TO FIND...

OH, NO. NOT AGAIN.

SCOTT? IT'S AWFULLY CHILLY OUT HERE. COME BACK TO BED. PLEASE?

I'LL BE IN IN A WHILE, MADDY. PLEASE GO ON BACK AND GET SOME SLEEP.

SCOTT, I'M... SORRY FOR SNAPPING AT YOU EARLIER... IT'S JUST THAT-- I'M FRIGHTENED! I DON'T WANT TO LOSE WHAT WE HAVE!

I UNDERSTAND THAT. I'M... JUST NOT EX-ACTLY SURE WHAT WE *DO* HAVE ANYMORE.

SCOTT, I'VE TRIED TO OVER-LOOK A LOT OF THINGS. I TRIED TO BE UNDERSTANDING WHEN YOU WEREN'T HERE FOR THE BABY'S BIRTH.

I KNOW. I SHOULD HAVE BEEN HERE.

I'VE EVEN TRIED TO DEAL WITH THE FACT THAT I RESEMBLE YOUR DEAD LOVER. IT'S NEVER BEEN AN EASY THING FOR ME TO LIVE WITH.

IT'S JEAN, ISN'T IT? YOU'RE THINKING ABOUT HER RIGHT NOW --AREN'T YOU?

YES.

THE NEXT MORNING, HIGH ABOVE THE ROCKY MOUNTAINS OF NEW MEXICO ONE OF THE WEALTHIEST MEN IN THE WORLD FLIES... *UNDER HIS OWN POWER!*

HE IS *WARREN WORTHINGTON III*-- ENTREPRENEUR, SOCIALITE, AND THE OBJECT OF MORE THAN ONE WOMAN'S DESIRE.

BUT THERE IS ALSO ANOTHER SIDE TO THIS MAN. HE IS ALSO KNOWN AS THE AVENGING *ANGEL*--MUTANT, FORMER X-MAN AND, UNTIL VERY RECENTLY, MEMBER OF AN ELITE SUPER-GROUP KNOWN AS THE NEW *DEFENDERS.* HOWEVER, WITH THE SUDDEN DEMISE OF THAT TEAM*, THE ANGEL'S PRIORITIES HAVE NARROWED! ALL THAT CON-CERNS HIM NOW IS THE REBUILDING OF HIS MOUNTAIN CHATEAU AND THE PURSUIT OF PURELY PERSONAL PLEASURES.

ON THIS MORNING, WARREN WORTHINGTON III'S LIFE AS AN ADVENTURER SEEMS DISTANT, INDEED.

*SEE DEFENDERS #152.

THE SAME CAN BE SAID FOR HIS FRIENDS AND FORMER COMRADES-IN-ARMS... HANK (*THE BEAST*) McCOY AND BOBBY (*THE ICEMAN*) DRAKE. TODAY IS THE DAY THESE THREE MUTANTS ATTEMPT TO *START* NEW--MORE *NORMAL*--LIVES!

POSITIVELY ENLIGHTENING, DRAKE! IT SAYS HERE THAT SIGNIFICANT BREAKTHROUGHS HAVE BEEN ACHIEVED IN ANALYZING THE PROCESS OF HOW ENTEROKINASE IS TRIGGERED IN THE INTESTINAL TRACT!

WELL--I'LL SLEEP EASIER, KNOWING THAT!

AND IF YOU'RE NOT GONNA HELP WITH THESE BAGS, I'LL GET THEM DOWNSTAIRS THE EASY WAY, VIA ONE HANDY-DANDY *ICE SLIDE!* GANGWAY!

HEY, FROSTBITE! WATCH OUT!

OF ALL THE CRETINOUS DISPLAYS--! IS YOUR *BRAIN* ON ICE, DRAKE? WARREN HAS JUST HAD THIS ABODE REFURBISHED AND YOU'VE LEFT *TWO HUNDRED POUNDS OF ICE* TO MELT IN HIS LIVING ROOM!

AW, COME OFF IT, HANK! OL' MONEYBAGS CAN USE IT AS AN EXCUSE TO REDECORATE EVERYTHING AGAIN! MORE THAN LIKELY HE'LL THANK ME! C'MON--LET'S GO SAY GOODBYE TO HIM AND CANDY!

OUTSIDE BY THE POOL, AMIDST THE DIN OF THE CURRENT RECONSTRUCTION...

HIYA, GUYS! ALL PACKED UP ALREADY?

ALAS, FAIR MS. SOUTHERN! OUR CHARIOT AWAITS TO WHISK US AWAY TO OUR NEW LIVES AMONGST THE CIVILIAN POPULACE!

WHAT HE SAID--SORTA! I'VE GOT TO REPORT TO MY NEW JOB AT THE ACCOUNTING FIRM BY NINE TOMORROW MORNING AND HANK HAS AN INTERVIEW WITH THE DEAN OF EMPIRE STATE UNIVERSITY ON TUESDAY! IF WE MISS OUR FLIGHTS, WE'LL BOTH BE IN DEEP DIP!

UH--CANDY? WE WERE HOPING THAT WARREN WOULD BE PRESENT TO SEE US OFF. IS HE--?

WELL...YOU KNOW HOW IT IS, HANK! HE'S PROBABLY A BIT DOWN ABOUT EVERYONE GIVING UP THE HERO BIZ.

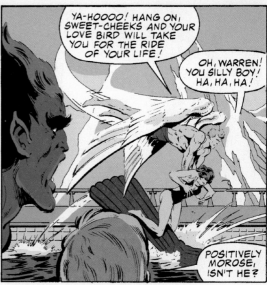

YA-HOOOO! HANG ON, SWEET-CHEEKS AND YOUR LOVE BIRD WILL TAKE YOU FOR THE RIDE OF YOUR LIFE!

OH, WARREN! YOU SILLY BOY! HA, HA, HA!

POSITIVELY MOROSE, ISN'T HE?

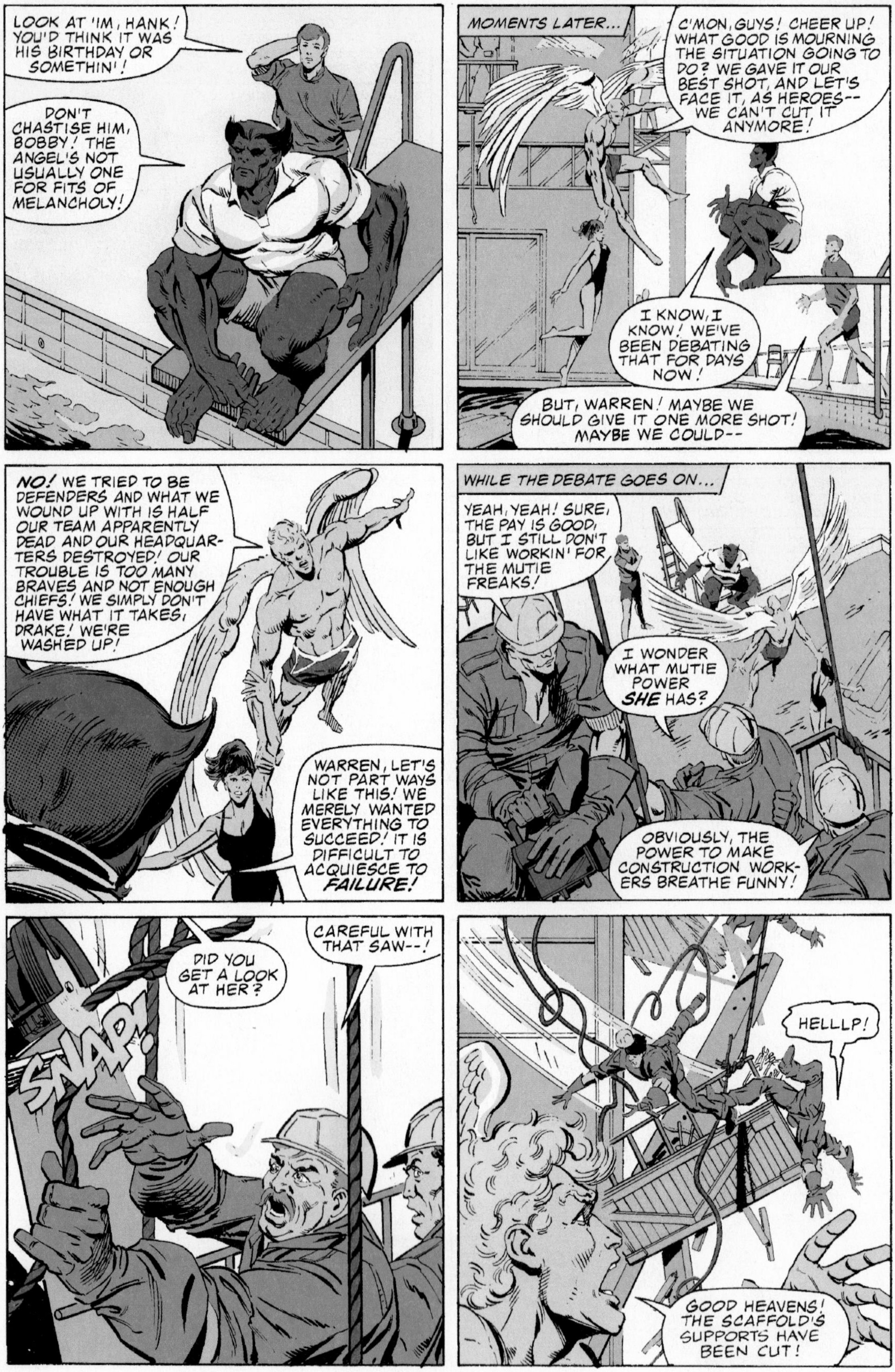
LOOK AT 'IM, HANK! YOU'D THINK IT WAS HIS BIRTHDAY OR SOMETHIN'!
DON'T CHASTISE HIM, BOBBY! THE ANGEL'S NOT USUALLY ONE FOR FITS OF MELANCHOLY!
MOMENTS LATER...
C'MON, GUYS! CHEER UP! WHAT GOOD IS MOURNING THE SITUATION GOING TO DO? WE GAVE IT OUR BEST SHOT, AND LET'S FACE IT, AS HEROES-- WE CAN'T CUT IT ANYMORE!
I KNOW, I KNOW! WE'VE BEEN DEBATING THAT FOR DAYS NOW!
BUT, WARREN! MAYBE WE SHOULD GIVE IT ONE MORE SHOT! MAYBE WE COULD--
NO! WE TRIED TO BE DEFENDERS AND WHAT WE WOUND UP WITH IS HALF OUR TEAM APPARENTLY DEAD AND OUR HEADQUARTERS DESTROYED! OUR TROUBLE IS TOO MANY BRAVES AND NOT ENOUGH CHIEFS! WE SIMPLY DON'T HAVE WHAT IT TAKES, DRAKE! WE'RE WASHED UP!
WARREN, LET'S NOT PART WAYS LIKE THIS! WE MERELY WANTED EVERYTHING TO SUCCEED! IT IS DIFFICULT TO ACQUIESCE TO FAILURE!
WHILE THE DEBATE GOES ON...
YEAH, YEAH! SURE, THE PAY IS GOOD, BUT I STILL DON'T LIKE WORKIN' FOR THE MUTIE FREAKS!
I WONDER WHAT MUTIE POWER SHE HAS?
OBVIOUSLY, THE POWER TO MAKE CONSTRUCTION WORKERS BREATHE FUNNY!
SNAP!
DID YOU GET A LOOK AT HER?
CAREFUL WITH THAT SAW--!
HELLLP!
GOOD HEAVENS! THE SCAFFOLD'S SUPPORTS HAVE BEEN CUT!

HANK! BOBBY! CLEAR THOSE MEN OFF OF THERE-- I'LL GET THAT GUY GOING OVER THE EDGE!

SPLOOSH

WITH UNBELIEVABLE SPEED, THE ANGEL RACES TO THE AID OF THE HAPLESS HARDHATS...

AND ICEMAN AND THE BEAST FOLLOW SUIT...

FEAR NOT, BRAVE BLUE-COLLAR! YOUR SAFETY IS ASSURED! ICEMAN, COULD YOU SEE FIT TO DEPOSIT THIS GENTLEMAN GENTLY ON TERRA FIRMA?

MEANWHILE I'LL TRY TO REACH THAT OTHER ROPE!

HE'S ALL YOURS, MY FRIGID FRIEND!

HANK! THAT GUIDE-ROPE--! IT'S NOT--

--SECURED!

OH... DRAT!

LOOK OUT BELOW!

KARREESH

KER-PLOOSH

67

ARE YOU GUYS OKAY?

OH, JUST SPLENDID! AN EXEMPLARY DISPLAY OF TEAMWORK, WOULDN'T YOU SAY?

AWW-- SHUT UP, HANK!

MINUTES LATER...

OKAY, I WANT YOU MEN TO KNOW THAT I'M RAISING YOUR HOURLY WAGE TO TIME-AND-A-HALF FOR THE DURATION!

HECK, FOR THAT WE'LL FALL OFF THE HOUSE EVERY HOUR ON THE HOUR!

I DON'T THINK THAT'LL BE NECESSARY, MEN! LET'S GET BACK TO IT, EH?

THE WORKERS DISPERSE, AND...

I SUPPOSE FATE DECIDED TO PUNCTUATE YOUR POINT, WARREN. WITHOUT A SCOTT SUMMERS OR A PROFESSOR XAVIER AROUND, WE'RE NOT MUCH TO WRITE HOME ABOUT.

WELL, DON'T BE TOO HARD ON YOURSELVES, HENRY. AFTER ALL, YOU DID SAVE THOSE MEN! THAT'S WHAT'S IMPORTANT!

LOOK, GUYS! YOU'RE THE BEST PEOPLE I KNOW AND I LOVE YA BOTH! BUT IT'S TIME WE ALL STARTED HAVING A LITTLE FUN! I'M THROUGH BEING A HERO! LET'S JUST TRY TO BE THE BEST AT WHATEVER COMES ALONG NEXT! COME ON-- I'LL WALK YOU TO YOUR CAR!

NOW-- YOU GUYS STAY IN TOUCH! I WANT TO KNOW HOW THINGS ARE GOING!

DON'T WORRY, WARREN! YOU'LL HEAR FROM US!

YEAH! EVERYTIME WE NEED TO BORROW SOME BUCKS!

THERE GO TWO OF THE BEST FELLOWS A MAN COULD KNOW!

YOU'RE NOT GOING TO GET ALL SENTIMENTAL ON ME NOW, ARE YOU?

MOI? NO WAY! GRAB ON TIGHT AND I'LL FLY YOU BACK TO THE HOUSE!

DO YOU WANT TO GO BACK TO THE POOL, HONEY?

AND CAUSE ANOTHER ACCIDENT BY LETTING THOSE GUYS CHECK OUT YOUR FABULOUS FRAME AGAIN? NO WAY! WHY DON'T WE... EH?

CANDY--HANK FORGOT ONE OF HIS BAGS! I HOPE THERE WASN'T ANYTHING IMPORTANT IN IT!

HEY, LOOK AT THIS! AN OLD PICTURE OF ALL OF US WHEN WE WERE FLEDGLING X-MEN!

BRRINNNGGG!

WOULD YOU GET THE PHONE, HON?

SURE THING, SWEETIE!

WARREN? IT'S REED RICHARDS OF THE FANTASTIC FOUR! IT SOUNDS URGENT!

OH, YOU WORRY TOO MUCH! HE AND HIS GROUP PROBABLY JUST WRECKED SOME OF MY MANHATTAN PROPERTY AGAIN!

HELLO? DOCTOR RICHARDS-- HOW ARE YOU? I'M--

WHAT!! THAT CAN'T BE! SURE, SURE! I'M ON MY WAY!

WARREN? WHAT'S WRONG? WHAT DID HE SAY?

NO TIME TO EXPLAIN, CANDY! I'VE GOT TO GET TO NEW YORK IMMEDIATELY!

BUT--YOU'RE NOT EVEN DRESSED! WHAT'S SO--

DO ME A FAVOR AND CALL THE AIRPORT! TELL VAUGHN TO HAVE THE SUPERSONIC FUELED AND READY IN TWENTY MINUTES!

HEY! YOU'RE NOT GOING TO LEAVE ME ALONE WITH A HOUSE FULL OF CONSTRUCTION WORKERS, ARE YOU?!

HMMMM! ON SECOND THOUGHT...

THE SAN DIEGO NAVAL YARD. THE MEDICAL FRIGATE, U.S.S. ESSEX, DOCKS AFTER MONTHS OF DUTY AT SEA...

C'MON, YA SWAB! SHORE LEAVE'S BEGUN AN' THE CLOCK'S RUNNIN'!

WHAT'S THE MATTER, CHIEF FISHER? DON'T YOU EVER TAKE IN THE VIEW?

JUST KIDDIN' SAILOR, AT EASE?

WHATSAY LET'S GET OUTTA HERE AND HAVE SOME FUN! I WANNA BE KNEE-DEEP IN MISDEMEANORS BY MIDNIGHT!

UH... S-SURE, CHIEF! I... JUST...

LATER, ON THE WASHINGTON STREET STRIP, THE SAILORS ENTER THE TRIPLE X BAR...

HEY, RUSTY, YA SEE DA BROAD ON DEM TASSLES?

Y-YES, SIR!

A FEW DRINKS LATER...

HEY, KID! I WANTCHA TO MEET AN OL' FRIEND O' MINE-- EMMA LA PORTE!

ENCHANTED, I'M SURE!

UH... P-PLEASED TO M-MEET YOU, MISS!

WELL, GOLLY, FISHER! I THINK HE'S SIMPLY ADORABLE!

Y-YOU MUST E-EXCUSE ME, MA'AM-- I'M N-NOT USED TO DRINKIN' ALL TH-THAT MUCH!

YEAH, EMMA! MAYBE A LITTLE NIGHT AIR WOULD STRAIGHTEN 'IM OUT!

EXCELLENT IDEA! COME ALONG, DARLING BOY!

I-I'M NOT S-SURE ABOUT THIS, M-MISS! I DON'T--

AW--GO AHEAD, KID! AN' DAT'S AN ORDER!

YOU HEARD HIM, SAILOR! YOU CAN'T DISOBEY A DIRECT ORDER, NOW, CAN YOU?

OUT IN THE ALLEYWAY--

NOW, MISS. Y-YOU'RE A N-NICE LADY AND ALL TH-THAT, BUT TH-THIS DON'T SEEM P-PROPER--!

LOOK, LOVERBOY! I'VE BEEN CALLED EVERYTHING IN THE BOOK, BUT--

-- I'VE NEVER BEEN "NICE"!

M-MISS... MMMM?

NO! I FEEL LIKE I'M BURNIN' UP! GET AWAY, PLEASE!? BEFORE IT'S--

--TOO LATE!

NOOOOO!

ARRRGHHH!

71

RIVETED BY THE HORRIFYING SIGHT BEFORE HIM, THE YOUNG SAILOR STANDS HELPLESS AS THE FLAMES CONSUME HIS WOULD-BE COMPANION...

MAKE IT STOP! SOMEBODY! PLEASE!

BLINDED BY PANIC, RUSTY RUNS OUT INTO THE STREETS, UNABLE TO CONTROL THE FLAMES THAT LEAP WILDLY FROM HIS FLESH...

LOOK AT THAT, WILL YA!

HELP! FIRE!

SOMEBODY HELP MEEEE!!

GIRLS GIRLS

FOUR AND A HALF HOURS AFTER RECEIVING REED RICHARDS'S MYSTERIOUS PHONE CALL, WARREN WORTHINGTON'S SLEEK, CUSTOM-BUILT CONCORDE TOUCHES DOWN AT NEW YORK'S J.F.K. AIRPORT.

FOR THE ANGEL, IT HAS SEEMED THE LONGEST FLIGHT OF HIS LIFE.

HE'S GOT TO BE HERE, SOMEWHERE! GOT TO GET THESE CLOTHES OFF-- NO TIME TO LOSE!

OH, MY HEAVEN! A WINGED MAN! I-I FEEL FAINT! THEOTIS--HELP!

DON'T FALL ON ME, WOMAN!

HEY! IT'S ONE OF THEM MUTIE FREAKS!

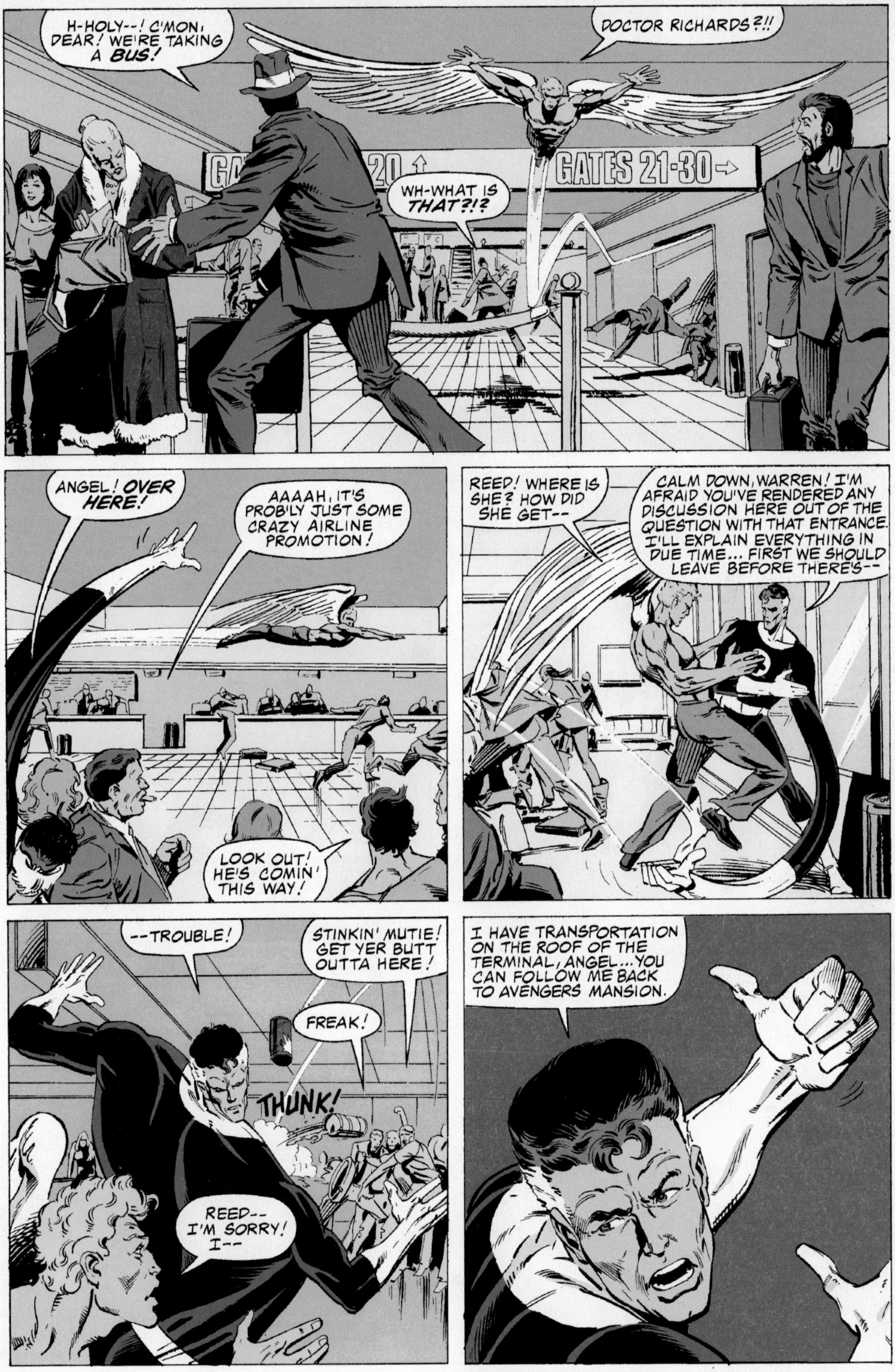
H-HOLY--! C'MON, DEAR! WE'RE TAKING A BUS!
DOCTOR RICHARDS?!!
GATES 21-30
WH-WHAT IS THAT?!?
ANGEL! OVER HERE!
AAAAH, IT'S PROB'LY JUST SOME CRAZY AIRLINE PROMOTION!
LOOK OUT! HE'S COMIN' THIS WAY!
REED! WHERE IS SHE? HOW DID SHE GET--
CALM DOWN, WARREN! I'M AFRAID YOU'VE RENDERED ANY DISCUSSION HERE OUT OF THE QUESTION WITH THAT ENTRANCE. I'LL EXPLAIN EVERYTHING IN DUE TIME... FIRST WE SHOULD LEAVE BEFORE THERE'S--
--TROUBLE!
STINKIN' MUTIE! GET YER BUTT OUTTA HERE!
FREAK!
THUNK!
REED-- I'M SORRY! I--
I HAVE TRANSPORTATION ON THE ROOF OF THE TERMINAL, ANGEL... YOU CAN FOLLOW ME BACK TO AVENGERS MANSION.

TWENTY MINUTES LATER, ON THE FRONT LAWN OF **AVENGERS MANSION**...

I-I CAN'T BELIEVE IT, REED! HOW COULD SHE HAVE SURVIVED? IT'S MIND-BOGGLING! *JEAN GREY-- ALIVE!?!*

I SURMISED THAT YOU MIGHT BE JUST WHAT SHE NEEDS RIGHT NOW... TO HELP HER **ADJUST**.

HELP **HER** ADJUST?!

INSIDE...

WHERE IS SHE, REED?

WARREN, PLEASE? CALM DOWN AND LET ME EXPLAIN A FEW THINGS TO YOU!

FAIR ENOUGH. MAY I SEE HER NOW, PLEASE?

OKAY, OKAY! I'M A BIT ON EDGE!

TOTALLY UNDERSTANDABLE CONSIDERING THE CIRCUMSTANCES. NOW, SHE'S BEEN THROUGH AN INCREDIBLE ORDEAL. ALTHOUGH SHE SEEMS TO BE IN GOOD SPIRITS, JEAN IS GOING TO NEED SOME TIME. TAKE IT SLOW.

OF COURSE.

MEANWHILE, OUTSIDE THE SAN DIEGO BAR, A PRISONER IS CAUTIOUSLY TRANSPORTED BY NAVAL PERSONNEL...

...AND THROUGHOUT THE CROWD THAT HAS GATHERED AROUND, ONE WORD IS OMINOUSLY WHISPERED.

MUTANT!

IT IS A WORD THAT RUSTY COLLINS HAD NEVER HEARD --UNTIL TODAY!

MUTIE SCUM! I HOPE DEY HANG YA!

C'MON, SON, INTO THE TRANSPORT!

'CAUSE O' YOU, EMMA MIGHT DIE! BUT YOU MUTIES DON'T GIVE A SQUAT ABOUT *REAL* PEOPLE, DO YA?

YA JUST HIDE AMONG US AN' KILL ANYONE WHO CROSSES YA! I'LL RIP YER LUNGS OUT!

CHILL OUT, CHIEF! THIS IS A JOB FOR THE AUTHORITES!

INTO THE VAN, SAILOR!

YA AIN'T GONNA GET AWAY WITH DIS, *FREAK!* I'M GONNA GET YA! *I SWEAR IT!*

RUSTY LOOKS INTO THE FACES OF THE CROWD FOR ANY SYMPATHETIC EYES! HE FINDS ONLY--

--FEAR!

FOUR O'CLOCK IN THE MORNING, E.S.T., FINDS WARREN WORTHINGTON IN THE POSH CONFINES OF A SUITE IN THE *WALDORF-ASTORIA HOTEL*...

WHAT AM I SUPPOSED TO DO? JEAN WANTS TO SEE SCOTT! IF I CALL HIM--HE'LL COME! I KNOW IT! BUT--

--WHAT WILL THIS DO TO HIS MARRIAGE? MADELYNE WILL NEVER BE ABLE TO DEAL WITH JEAN'S RESURRECTION!

FACE IT, WARREN! PART OF YOU IS HOPING HE *WON'T COME!* IT COULD BE A CHANCE FOR YOU AND JEAN TO--

SPIT! I DON'T KNOW WHAT TO DO!

AFTER HOURS OF SOUL-SEARCHING, HE KNOWS THAT HE TRULY HAS *NO CHOICE!*

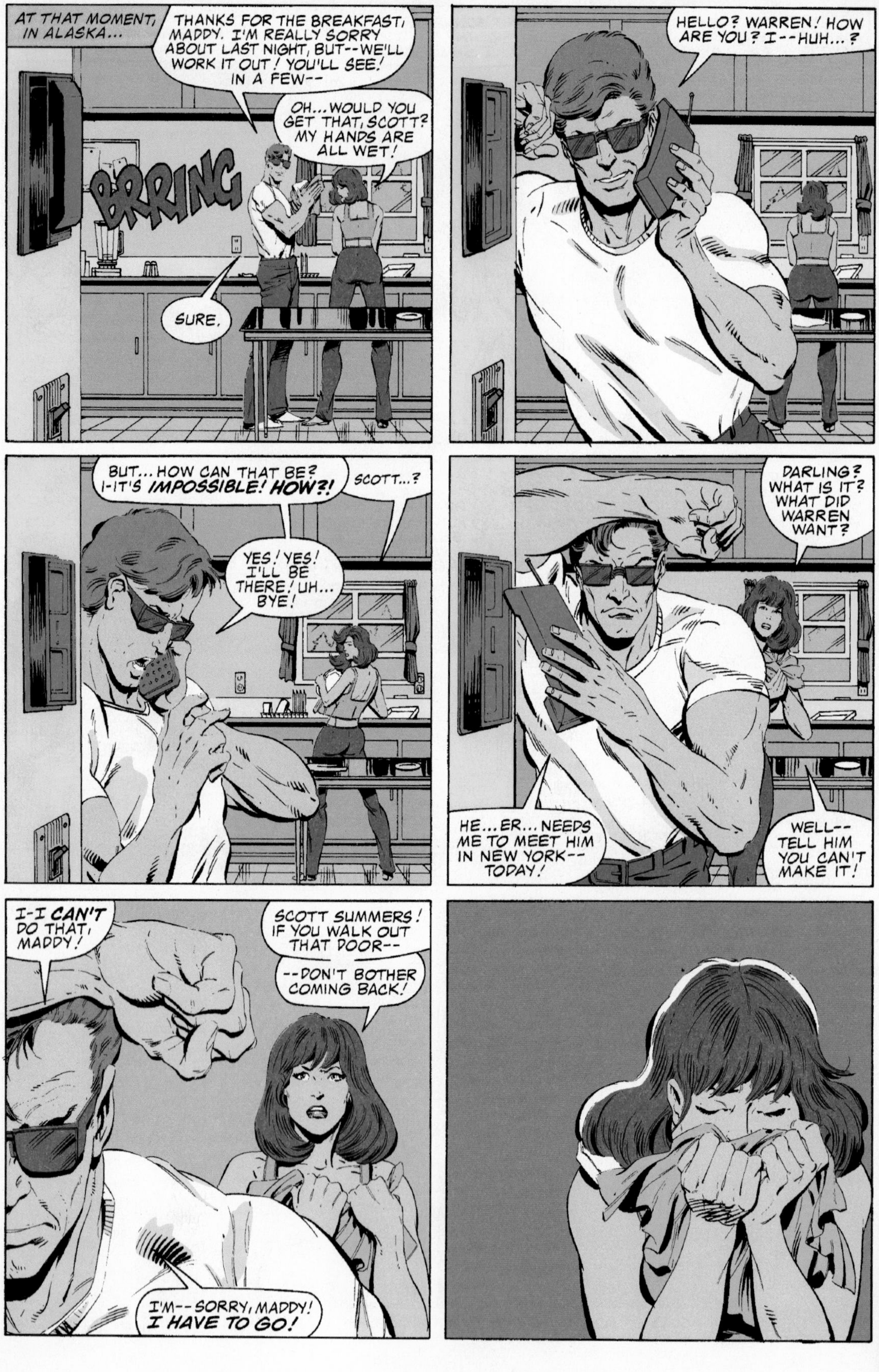
AT THAT MOMENT, IN ALASKA...
THANKS FOR THE BREAKFAST, MADDY. I'M REALLY SORRY ABOUT LAST NIGHT, BUT--WE'LL WORK IT OUT! YOU'LL SEE! IN A FEW--
OH...WOULD YOU GET THAT, SCOTT? MY HANDS ARE ALL WET!
BRRING
SURE.
HELLO? WARREN! HOW ARE YOU? I--HUH...?
BUT...HOW CAN THAT BE? I-IT'S IMPOSSIBLE! HOW?!
SCOTT...?
YES! YES! I'LL BE THERE! UH... BYE!
DARLING? WHAT IS IT? WHAT DID WARREN WANT?
HE...ER...NEEDS ME TO MEET HIM IN NEW YORK-- TODAY!
WELL-- TELL HIM YOU CAN'T MAKE IT!
I-I CAN'T DO THAT, MADDY!
SCOTT SUMMERS! IF YOU WALK OUT THAT DOOR--
--DON'T BOTHER COMING BACK!
I'M--SORRY, MADDY! I HAVE TO GO!

TWELVE HOURS LATER, SCOTT SUMMERS ARRIVES AT THE WALDORF-ASTORIA HOTEL IN NEW YORK.

A RESIDENCE ALMOST EXCLUSIVELY FOR THE FAMOUS AND WEALTHY, THE WALDORF IS A MONUMENT TO A LIFESTYLE SCOTT KNOWS LITTLE OF...AND AT THIS MOMENT, CARES NOTHING ABOUT.

THE HOTEL ELEVATOR REACHES THE ELEVENTH FLOOR, THE DOOR OPENS, AND SCOTT DISCOVERS...

HOLD IT RIGHT THERE, MISTER! THIS FLOOR IS RESTRICTED TO--

BACK OFF, GUYS! HE'S THE SUMMERS GUY MISTER WORTHINGTON'S WAITIN' FOR. LET 'IM PASS!

THANK YOU.

WOULD ONE OF YOU PLEASE EXPLAIN WHAT'S GOING ON HERE?

JUST DOING OUR JOB, SIR. MISTER WORTHINGTON WILL ANSWER ANY QUESTIONS YOU HAVE.

ONCE INSIDE THE SUITE...

WARREN, WHAT ARE ALL THOSE RENT-A-COPS DOING OUT-SIDE?

IS THAT ANY WAY TO GREET AN OLD FRIEND, SCOTT? I HIRED THOSE GUARDS TO INSURE OUR PRIVACY. YOU CAN'T BE TOO CAREFUL WITH ALL THE MUTANT HATERS AROUND NOWADAYS!

WHERE IS SHE, WARREN?

SHE'S IN THE NEXT ROOM. SHE'S BEEN WAITING FOR YOU!

HOW MUCH... HAVE YOU TOLD HER?

NOT A THING, OL' BUDDY! I'M AFRAID I HAD TO LEAVE THAT TO YOU!

SLOWLY, SCOTT OPENS THE DOOR AND...

OH, MY GOD! IT IS JEAN!!

SCOTT!

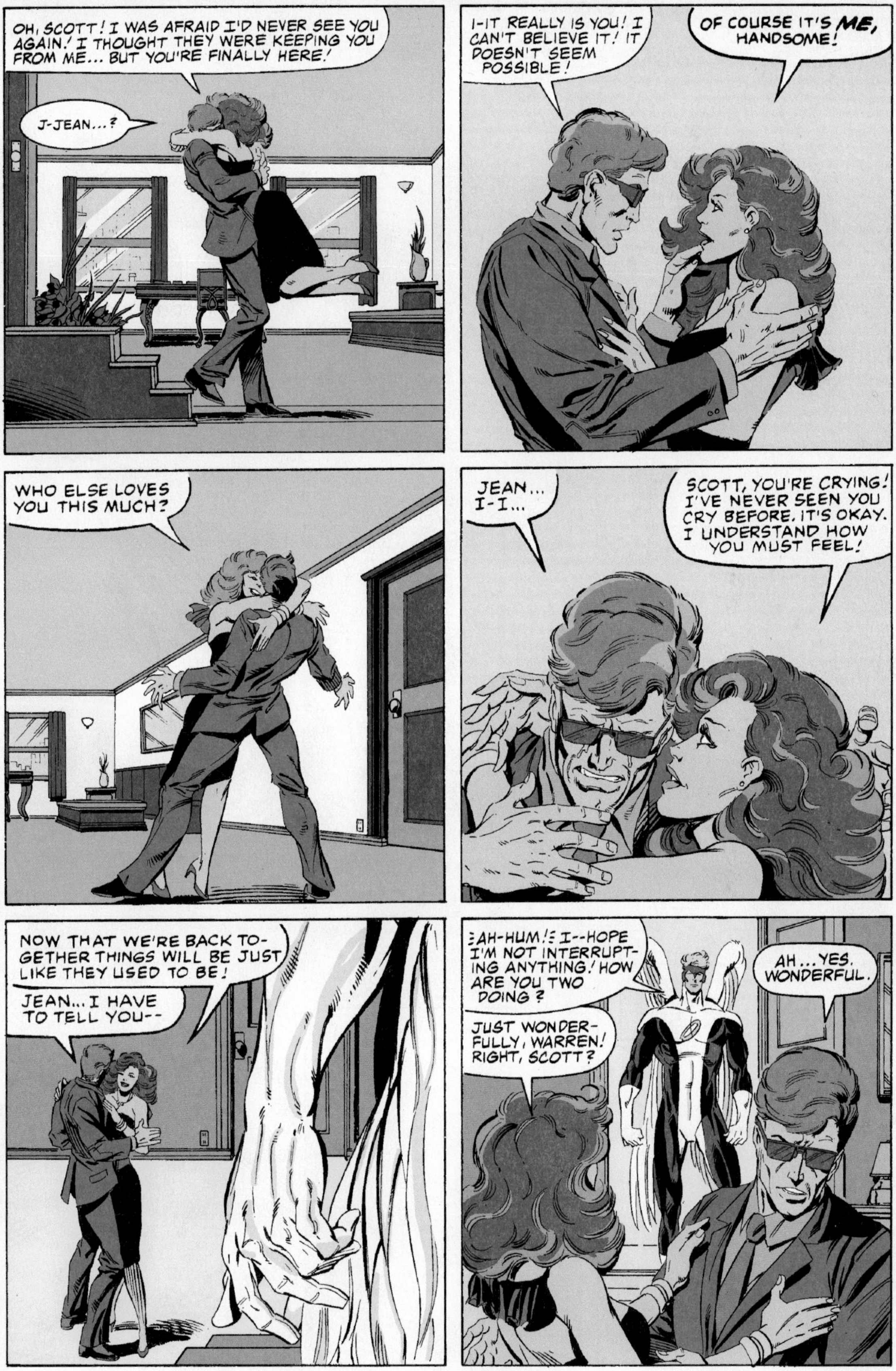
OH, SCOTT! I WAS AFRAID I'D NEVER SEE YOU AGAIN! I THOUGHT THEY WERE KEEPING YOU FROM ME... BUT YOU'RE FINALLY HERE!
J-JEAN...?
I-IT REALLY IS YOU! I CAN'T BELIEVE IT! IT DOESN'T SEEM POSSIBLE!
OF COURSE IT'S ME, HANDSOME!
WHO ELSE LOVES YOU THIS MUCH?
JEAN... I-I...
SCOTT, YOU'RE CRYING! I'VE NEVER SEEN YOU CRY BEFORE. IT'S OKAY. I UNDERSTAND HOW YOU MUST FEEL!
NOW THAT WE'RE BACK TOGETHER THINGS WILL BE JUST LIKE THEY USED TO BE!
JEAN... I HAVE TO TELL YOU--
AH-HUM! I--HOPE I'M NOT INTERRUPTING ANYTHING! HOW ARE YOU TWO DOING?
JUST WONDERFULLY, WARREN! RIGHT, SCOTT?
AH... YES. WONDERFUL.

ISN'T IT GREAT!? I MEAN -- THE THREE OF US ALL TOGETHER LIKE THIS.

IT'S MORE THAN SOME OF US COULD HAVE EVER HOPED FOR, JEAN!

WARREN, I AM CURIOUS ABOUT HOW JEAN SURVIVED! I MEAN -- I THOUGHT YOU DIED!

WELL -- NOT EXACTLY, SCOTT! I'LL TRY TO EXPLAIN IT AS DOCTOR RICHARDS DID!

I'M ALL EARS.

"IT STARTED WHEN THE NEW X-MEN BECAME INVOLVED IN A SKIRMISH IN OUTER SPACE.

"JEAN TOOK IT UPON HERSELF TO PILOT A DAMAGED CRAFT EARTHWARD, ALTHOUGH DOING SO MEANT HER CERTAIN DEATH FROM EXPOSURE TO RADIATION.

"THE SHUTTLE CRASHED VIOLENTLY AND SANK TO THE BOTTOM OF JAMAICA BAY!

"EVERYONE ABOARD MADE IT TO THE SURFACE WITH THE EXCEPTION OF JEAN."

"WHY ARE YOU TELLING ME THIS, WARREN? I WAS THERE!"

"PLEASE, SCOTT, ALLOW ME TO CONTINUE. YOU'LL SOON UNDERSTAND.

"EVERYONE HAD ASSUMED THAT JEAN HAD PERISHED IN THE CRASH. AND JUST AS THE GROUP WAS ABANDONING ALL HOPE, THE WATER BEGAN TO CHURN AND BOIL...

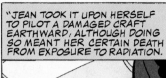

"... AND JEAN GREY WAS REBORN AS THE *PHOENIX!*

"AT LEAST WE ALL *THOUGHT* IT WAS JEAN!

"FOR MONTHS LIFE CONTINUED AS NORMAL-- I MEAN, AS NORMAL AS IT COULD EVER BE WITH THE X-MEN...

"BUT THEN, WITHOUT EXPLANATION, PHOENIX'S TRANSFORMATION APPARENTLY BEGAN TO EXACT A HEAVY TOLL ON HER! THE GROWING COSMIC FORCES WITHIN HER EVENTUALLY POSSESSED HER UNTIL SHE BECAME THE EVIL STAR-CONSUMING *DARK PHOENIX!*

"HER POWER THREATENED TO DESTROY THE WORLD! BUT REALIZING WHAT SHE HAD BECOME, SHE DESTROYED HERSELF IN ORDER TO SAVE THE GALAXY!

"SHE DIED A *HERO.*

HER HUMANITY HAD, IN THE END, DEFEATED HER CORRUPTED POWER!

THE POOR CREATURE!

WHY ARE YOU PEOPLE TALKING LIKE THE PHOENIX WAS SOMEONE ELSE? I DON'T UNDER--

THAT'S WHY I WAS GIVING YOU THE BUILD-UP, SCOTT! IT'S IMPORTANT YOU KNOW *EXACTLY* WHAT REALLY HAPPENED!

I'M LISTENING, WARREN!

"WELL, A WEEK AGO THE AVENGERS WERE CALLED TO INVESTIGATE A STRANGE OCCURRENCE AT THE BOTTOM OF JAMAICA BAY! IT WAS THERE THAT THEY DISCOVERED A MYSTERIOUS OBJECT RADIATING GREAT ENERGIES!

"THEY RETURNED, WITH THE CAPSULE-LIKE OBJECT, TO AVENGERS' MANSION! THERE, REED RICHARDS BEGAN TO ELECTRONICALLY PROBE THE CAPSULE TO DISCOVER ITS ORIGIN.

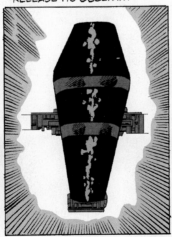

"APPARENTLY, THOSE PROBES ACTIVATED SOME MECHANISM, CAUSING THE CAPSULE TO RELEASE ITS OCCUPANT--

"--JEAN GREY!

"YOU SEE, SCOTT--THE PHOENIX WAS A *SEPARATE* ENTITY THAT HAD PERFECTLY DUPLICATED JEAN'S BODY AND PERSONALITY-- *TOO* PERFECTLY, SINCE JEAN'S HEROISM CAUSED THE ENTITY'S SELF-DESTRUCTION!

81

ALL THIS WHILE JEAN WAS LEFT IN STASIS IN THE CAPSULE UNTIL HER EXTENSIVE INJURIES HEALED!

THE ONLY NEGATIVE OUTCOME FROM THE WHOLE ORDEAL IS JEAN'S LOSS OF HER TELEPATHIC ABILITIES!

ODDLY ENOUGH-- MY TELEKINETIC POWERS HAVE BEEN INCREASED DRAMATICALLY BY THE EXPERIENCE!

IT'S-- SIMPLY INCREDIBLE! I-I'M AT A LOSS FOR WORDS!

NOW THAT WE'VE EXPLAINED MY STORY-- I HAVE A FEW MILLION QUESTIONS TO ASK BOTH OF YOU!

I'VE BEEN DOING SOME READING --CATCHING UP ON WHAT'S HAPPENING IN THE WORLD... DO YOU GUYS *KNOW* WHAT'S GOING ON OUT THERE? MUTANTKIND IS ALMOST ON THE VERGE OF EXTINCTION! IF SOMETHING ISN'T DONE--

I KNOW. THINGS ARE *NOT* GOOD FOR US RIGHT NOW.

"AREN'T GOOD?!" IT LOOKS LIKE IT'S OPEN SEASON ON MUTANTS! EVERY MAGAZINE, EVERY NEWSPAPER, EVERY T.V. SHOW HAS SOMETHING TO SAY AGAINST MUTANTS!

WE MUST *DO SOMETHING* TO PROTECT OUR OWN KIND!

I KNOW WE CAN'T RETURN TO THE X-MEN! THE AVENGERS EXPLAINED TO ME THAT *PROFESSOR XAVIER'S* GONE AND OUR ARCH-ENEMY *MAGNETO* HAS TAKEN CHARGE! BUT WE MUST BE ABLE TO DO SOMETHING-- *ANYTHING!* FORM *OUR OWN* GROUP, IF NOTHING ELSE!

IT'S-- NOT THAT CUT AND DRIED, JEANNIE! YOU SEE--

--I'VE GIVEN UP THE HERO BIZ! I'M TIRED OF THE WHOLE GOOD GUY-BAD GUY ROUTINE!

WHAT?

I DON'T BELIEVE YOU! HOW CAN YOU TURN YOUR BACK ON WHAT'S HAPPENING OUTSIDE?

SCOTT! TALK SOME SENSE INTO HIM! YOU'VE ALWAYS BEEN THE LEADER OF THE GROUP! HE'LL LISTEN TO YOU!

ER--WELL--I THINK I KNOW HOW WARREN FEELS, JEAN! I RECENTLY TRIED TO TAKE OVER AS LEADER OF THE X-MEN BUT I--ER--I COULDN'T CUT IT! I'VE--AH--RETIRED AS WELL, MORE OR LESS!

WHAT IS WRONG WITH YOU?!!

YOU ACTUALLY TRIED TO WORK WITH MAGNETO? THE MAN WHO WAS TRYING TO KILL US AT EVERY TURN WHEN WE WERE GROWING UP?

WELL...I...

BOY--YOU GUYS MAKE ME SICK!! WHAT'S HAPPENED TO YOUR COMMITMENT TO PROFESSOR X'S DREAM? ALL I KNOW IS--

--I'M NOT GOING TO STAND AROUND TWIDDLING MY THUMBS WHILE OUR KIND IS TOTALLY WIPED FROM THE FACE OF THE EARTH!

KER-THOOM

JEAN! WAIT! DON'T DO THIS!

C'MON, SCOTT! WE MUST GO AFTER HER! SHE'S NOT READY TO DEAL WITH THE OUTSIDE WORLD, YET!

HAVING LOWERED THE DEBRIS GENTLY TO THE PAVEMENT WITH HER TELEKINETIC POWER, JEAN GREY EFFORTLESSLY MANEUVERS ABOUT THE MANHATTAN SKY, WHILE--

--BACK AT THE SUITE...

EVERYTHING'S CONFUSED... MAKES NO SENSE...

WHAT'S WITH YOU? GRAB HOLD AND WE'LL GO AFTER HER!

I...CAN'T! SO MUCH... NOT RIGHT... ALL SCREWED UP...

WELL--TO BLAZES WITH YOU THEN!

IN A DESERTED ALLEYWAY...

WAY TO GO, JEANNIE! YOU LET THAT RED-HEADED TEMPER GET THE BEST OF YOU! I ONLY WISH I KNEW WHAT I WAS GOING TO DO NEXT! NO HOME, NO JOB, AND--

BEAUTIFUL LANDING, KID! COULDN'T HAVE DONE IT BETTER MYSELF!

WARREN! HOW DID YOU--?

YOU FORGOT THAT MY WINGS AREN'T THE ONLY THINGS THAT'RE LIKE AN EAGLE'S! I SAW YOU FROM TEN BLOCKS AWAY!

SO YOU FOUND ME! I DON'T THINK WE HAVE ANYTHING MORE TO DISCUSS!

BUT I THINK WE *DO!* YOU SEE-- I THOUGHT ABOUT IT AND I THINK YOU'RE RIGHT!

SO-- WHAT DO WE DO?

WE MAKE PLANS! AND I HAVE AN IDEA!

TWO WEEKS LATER, IN THE DEAN'S OFFICE OF BOSTON'S HARVARD MEDICAL SCHOOL--

DR. MCCOY-- I'M SORRY TO HAVE KEPT YOU WAITING SO LONG! DO COME IN!

NO NEED TO APOLOGIZE, DEAN HAUSER! IT GAVE ME AN OPPORTUNITY TO DO SOME LIGHT READING!! HAVE *YOU* EVER READ "WAR AND PEACE"?

≡AHEM≡--WELL, YOUR RESUMÉ *IS* IMPRESSIVE--INCLUDING YOUR SCIENTIFIC CONSULTANT POSITION WITH THE--≡AHEM≡--AVENGERS, IS IT?

Y-YES--≡AHEM≡--I'M SURE.

YES, SIR! A TERRIFIC GROUP OF PEOPLE TO WORK WITH!

I MUST SAY I'M TERRIBLY ANXIOUS TO START WITH YOUR RESEARCH DEPARTMENT IMMEDIATELY, SIR!

HENRY--ALLOW ME TO BE FRANK. I'VE RECEIVED A--≡AHEM≡--PETITION FROM THE OTHER FACULTY MEMBERS, AND IT WOULD APPEAR THEY FEEL THAT HIRING SOMEONE ON THE STAFF WHO IS A--≡AHEM≡--MUTANT WOULD SERIOUSLY JEOPARDIZE THE REPUTATION OF OUR SCHOOL! PICKETS-- AND PROTEST MARCHES--NASTY BUSINESS, LET ME ASSURE YOU! I'M AFRAID I MUST THEREFORE *REJECT* YOUR APPLICATION!

PERHAPS YOU COULD TRY YALE, OR--

"REJECT?!" OF ALL THE UNMITIGATED--! THIS IS THE *FIFTEENTH* INTERVIEW I'VE BEEN ON AND ALL I'VE ENCOUNTERED ARE PETTY BIGOTRIES! WELL, YOU CAN TAKE YOUR CRUMMY RESEARCH FACILITIES AND LODGE THEM-- LODGE THEM-- *YOU KNOW WHERE!* I'VE HAD ENOUGH!

TAKING OFF YOUR CLOTHES--IN MY OFFICE?

YOU CAN KEEP THEM-- *AND YOUR SCHOOL!*

McCOY! DON'T DO THIS! SOME- ONE MIGHT SEE! THINK OF *MY* REPUTATION!

I'M GOING TO LOCATE A BEAUTIFUL DESERT ISLAND SOMEWHERE AND THINK ABOUT *NOTHING!*

HANK McCOY? MAY I HAVE A WORD WITH YOU?

UNLESS YOU'RE GONNA OFFER ME PAYING WORK, I'VE NOTHING TO SAY TO YOU, MISTER!

WELL--AS A MATTER OF FACT, THERE IS PAYMENT INVOLVED-- WARREN WORTHINGTON SENT ME!

WARREN? IN THAT CASE--LEAD THE WAY!

LATER THAT DAY, AT THE ACCOUNTING FIRM OF HARRAS, ANDERSON AND BROWN, BOBBY DRAKE GOES ABOUT THE MUNDANE TASK OF AUDITING INVOICES AND COUNTING THE MINUTES UNTIL HIS LUNCH BREAK...

HEY, DRAKE! CALL FOR YOU ON LINE FOUR!

THANKS, ELIOT!

SO-- AS I WAS SAYING--

WHAT? SURE, SURE! TELL WARREN I'LL BE THERE! *RIGHT AWAY!*

--THIS WHOLE MUTANT HYSTERIA IS A FABRICATION OF THE MEDIA! LIKE U.F.O.S AND SUCH NONSENSE!

YOU'RE WRONG, IRV! I'VE *SEEN* THEM ON THE NEWS!

DON'T BE RIDICULOUS! THEY DON'T--! *YIPES!!*

YA-HOO! *THE ICEMAN COMETH AGAIN!*

YOU WERE SAYING, IRV?

SIX HOURS LATER, ON MANHATTAN'S LOWER EAST SIDE, A SLEEK, PROTOTYPE HELICOPTER MAKES ITS DESCENT ONTO A CHOICE PIECE OF WATERFRONT PROPERTY...TWO BEWILDERED PASSENGERS ARE DISCHARGED AND CAUTIOUSLY ENTER THE IMMENSE STRUCTURE LOOMING BEFORE THEM...

ONCE INSIDE...

HOLY CROW! WILLYA LOOK AT THE *SIZE* OF THIS PLACE!

WARREN? WHAT IS THIS ALL ABOUT? DID YOU CALL US HERE JUST TO SHOW OFF ANOTHER ONE OF YOUR RECENT REAL ESTATE ACQUISITIONS?

HANK, BOBBY--YOU ARE NOW STANDING IN THE BRAND-SPANKING-NEW HEADQUARTERS BUILDING OF MY NEW *CORPORATION!*

BUT THAT'S NOT THE REASON I CALLED YOU BOYS HERE.

THEN WHAT'S THE SCOOP? WHY ALL OF THIS SECRET SUMMONING?

GUYS--GET READY FOR THE *BIGGEST* SURPRISE OF YOUR LIFE!

GET ON WITH IT, MAN! WHAT'S GOING ON?!!

I THINK HE'S REFERRING TO ME, BOYS!

WHA--?!

HANK! BOBBY! GUESS WHO'S BACK!

J-J-JEANIE...? C-CAN IT B-BE...?

J-JEAN? I-IS IT R-REALLY YOU?

YOU'D BETTER BELIEVE IT, FUZZ BALL!

YAHOO! I CAN'T BELIEVE IT!

THEN, AFTER WHAT SEEMS LIKE AN ENDLESS BARRAGE OF QUESTIONS FROM THE ICEMAN AND THE BEAST...

THIS IS GREAT--JUST GREAT! THERE'S SO MUCH I MUST TELL YOU!

WE'LL HAVE PLENTY OF TIME TO DISCUSS ALL THIS LATER! RIGHT NOW WE NEED YOUR HELP DESPERATELY!

THE JOYOUS MOMENTS OF REUNION SEGUE SLOWLY INTO EXPLANATIONS AS THE TWO NEWCOMERS ARE TOLD THE TALE OF JEAN GREY'S FANTASTIC ORDEAL!

IT'S SCOTT! HE...ER...DISAPPEARED A FEW WEEKS AGO! WE HAD A FEW CHOICE WORDS AND--WELL, WE WERE HOPING YOU BOYS COULD FIND HIM--QUICKLY! THERE'S STILL A LOT OF WORK JEAN AND I MUST DO HERE!

AND EVERYTHING WE'RE TRYING TO DO HERE DEPENDS ON SCOTT'S PARTICIPATION!

WAIT A MINUTE! WHAT ARE YOU TALKING ABOUT? WHAT ARE WE TRYING TO DO?

NEVER MIND THAT, BOBBY! IF SCOTT'S SEEN JEAN--TALKED WITH HER--! WE GET THE PICTURE, WARREN! DON'T YOU WORRY, WE'LL FIND HIM!

DAWN ON JAMAICA BAY! THE SITE OF JEAN GREY'S "DEATH" AND THE BIRTH OF A PHOENIX...

...THE PLACE WHERE SCOTT SUMMERS' WOES BEGAN.

SCOTT...?

LEAVE ME ALONE, McCOY!

SCOTTY, WE'VE BEEN LOOKING ALL OVER FOR YOU! I HAD A HUNCH YOU MIGHT BE HERE!

YOU ALWAYS WERE THE CLEVER ONE, EH? SO... YOU'VE FOUND ME! NOW, LET ME BE!

SCOTT, WE'RE YOUR FRIENDS, MAN! WE JUST WANT TO HELP! WHAT'S WRONG?

M-MY WHOLE LIFE, DRAKE, THAT'S WHAT'S WRONG!

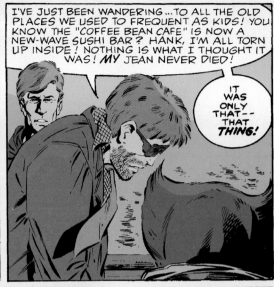

I'VE JUST BEEN WANDERING ...TO ALL THE OLD PLACES WE USED TO FREQUENT AS KIDS! YOU KNOW THE "COFFEE BEAN CAFE" IS NOW A NEW-WAVE SUSHI BAR? HANK, I'M ALL TORN UP INSIDE! NOTHING IS WHAT I THOUGHT IT WAS! MY JEAN NEVER DIED!

IT WAS ONLY-- THAT THING!

I-I EVEN MOURNED FOR JEAN... RESOLVED MYSELF ...!

HOW CAN I EVEN FACE HER--

WHAT ABOUT MADELYNE? HOW DO I EXPLAIN HOW I FEEL TO HER? HOW CAN I TELL HER ANY OF THIS?

YOU'RE STILL IN LOVE WITH JEAN?

I-I...

SCOTT! I CAN'T PRETEND TO KNOW WHAT YOU'RE FEELING! BUT THERE IS SOMETHING I DO KNOW! YOU CAN'T RUN AWAY FROM YOUR PROBLEMS, MAN! YOU CAN'T RUN FROM ANY OF US! WE'VE ALWAYS BEEN LIKE A FAMILY AND --

--THAT HASN'T CHANGED!

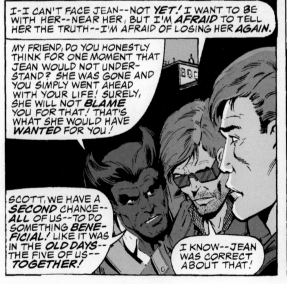

I-I CAN'T FACE JEAN--NOT YET! I WANT TO BE WITH HER--NEAR HER, BUT I'M AFRAID TO TELL HER THE TRUTH--I'M AFRAID OF LOSING HER AGAIN.

MY FRIEND, DO YOU HONESTLY THINK FOR ONE MOMENT THAT JEAN WOULD NOT UNDERSTAND? SHE WAS GONE AND YOU SIMPLY WENT AHEAD WITH YOUR LIFE! SURELY, SHE WILL NOT BLAME YOU FOR THAT! THAT'S WHAT SHE WOULD HAVE WANTED FOR YOU!

SCOTT, WE HAVE A SECOND CHANCE-- ALL OF US--TO DO SOMETHING BENEFICIAL! LIKE IT WAS IN THE OLD DAYS-- THE FIVE OF US-- TOGETHER!

I KNOW--JEAN WAS CORRECT ABOUT THAT!

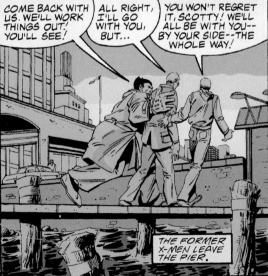

COME BACK WITH US! WE'LL WORK THINGS OUT! YOU'LL SEE!

ALL RIGHT, I'LL GO WITH YOU, BUT...

YOU WON'T REGRET IT, SCOTTY! WE'LL ALL BE WITH YOU-- BY YOUR SIDE--THE WHOLE WAY!

THE FORMER X-MEN LEAVE THE PIER.

THE NEXT DAY, A RELATIVE CALM HAS FALLEN OVER THE COMPLEX HOUSING THE FORMER X-MEN--

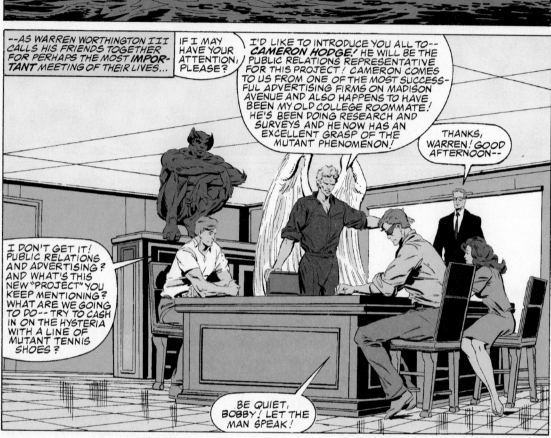

--AS WARREN WORTHINGTON III CALLS HIS FRIENDS TOGETHER FOR PERHAPS THE MOST *IMPORTANT* MEETING OF THEIR LIVES...

IF I MAY HAVE YOUR ATTENTION, PLEASE?

I'D LIKE TO INTRODUCE YOU ALL TO-- *CAMERON HODGE!* HE WILL BE THE PUBLIC RELATIONS REPRESENTATIVE FOR THIS PROJECT! CAMERON COMES TO US FROM ONE OF THE MOST SUCCESSFUL ADVERTISING FIRMS ON MADISON AVENUE AND ALSO HAPPENS TO HAVE BEEN MY OLD COLLEGE ROOMMATE! HE'S BEEN DOING RESEARCH AND SURVEYS AND HE NOW HAS AN EXCELLENT GRASP OF THE MUTANT PHENOMENON!

THANKS, WARREN! *GOOD AFTERNOON*--

I DON'T GET IT! PUBLIC RELATIONS AND ADVERTISING? AND WHAT'S THIS NEW "PROJECT" YOU KEEP MENTIONING? WHAT ARE WE GOING TO DO-- TRY TO CASH IN ON THE HYSTERIA WITH A LINE OF MUTANT TENNIS SHOES?

BE QUIET, BOBBY! LET THE MAN SPEAK!

THANK YOU. NOW--ALLOW ME TO EXPLAIN EXACTLY WHAT WE HAVE COME UP WITH...

OUR PROBLEM, SIMPLY STATED, IS TO LOCATE AND SOMEHOW GAIN THE *TRUST* OF THE GROWING POPULATION OF MUTANTS IN EVERYDAY SOCIETY.

AFTER PROVIDING THEM WITH THE NECESSARY TRAINING TO *CONTROL* THEIR...UM... *GIFTS* WE CAN RETURN THEM TO SOCIETY TO LIVE QUIET, SAFE, PRODUCTIVE LIVES.

AND THANKS TO MY YEARS OF P.R. AND AD EXPERIENCE, I BELIEVE WE HAVE DEVELOPED A VIABLE SYSTEM FOR DEFUSING THE *PROBLEM* OF MUTANT HYSTERIA BY TURNING IT *UPON* ITSELF!

THIS SOUNDS A LOT LIKE WHAT PROFESSOR X USED TO TELL US!

EVERYDAY, MORE MUTANTS ARE BORN INTO A WORLD WHERE THEY MUST LIVE IN CONSTANT FEAR! FEAR OF THE HUMAN POPULACE THAT SEES THEM AS A *THREAT,* AS WELL AS FEAR OF THEIR OWN, SPECIAL POWERS THAT THEY DON'T FULLY UNDERSTAND OR CAN'T CONTROL.

WE KNOW ALL THAT, MISTER HODGE! WHAT IS IT THAT YOU PROPOSE?

OUR ORGANIZATION WILL CAPITALIZE ON HUMAN BEINGS' *DISTRUST* OF MUTANTS BY POSING AS A *MUTANT DETERRENT AGENCY.*

WHAT?

ARE YOU GUYS SERIOUS?

PLEASE-- ALLOW ME TO CONTINUE!

PEOPLE THAT SUSPECT A MUTANT MENACE WILL CALL OUR TOLL-FREE NUMBER TO REPORT AN INCIDENT! WE WILL THEN, IN THE GUISE OF A TEAM OF PSYCHOLOGISTS AND SCIENTISTS, *INVESTIGATE* THE SUBJECT! IN REALITY, OUR TRUE GOAL IS TO ISOLATE AND PROTECT THE PEOPLE WHO POSSESS THE *X-FACTOR MUTATION* IN THEIR GENETIC MAKE-UP.

APPROPRIATELY, THE NAME OUR ORGANIZATION WILL BE KNOWN BY IS--

X-FACTOR

MUTANT INVESTIGATIONS AND *RESOLUTIONS!* NO NEED TO BE FEARFUL ANY LONGER! OUR SKILLED TEAM OF *EXPERTS* WILL AID YOU IN FINDING THE ANSWERS TO ONE OF THE MOST URGENT PROBLEMS OF OUR TIME! CALL OUR TOLL FREE NUMBER! OPERATORS STANDING BY! *VISA* AND *MASTERCARD* ACCEPTED!

DON'T WAIT UNTIL IT'S *TOO LATE!*

THIS IS A SAMPLE OF THE PRINT AD FOR OUR SERVICE! AND IF YOU'LL PLEASE WATCH THE MONITOR, YOU'LL SEE OUR NEW TELEVISION SPOT!

EVERY DAY, MORE AND MORE PEOPLE ARE THREATENED BY THE DREADED MUTANT MENACE. LAW ENFORCEMENT OFFICIALS ARE INEFFECTIVE AND SKEPTICAL WHILE *YOU* REMAIN A HELPLESS TARGET OF THESE STRANGE BEINGS! YOU'VE HEARD ABOUT THEM--THEY LIVE IN SECRET AND PLAN TO DESTROY THE VERY LIVES OF US *NORMAL* PEOPLE! BUT NOW THERE IS HELP! NOW THERE IS--

--X-FACTOR! PROFESSIONAL INVESTIGATORS, WHO, WITH THE HELP OF TODAY'S TECHNOLOGY, CAN PROTECT YOU AND YOUR FAMILY FROM THIS UNSEEN MENACE! IF YOU SUSPECT *ANYONE* OF MUTANT ACTIVITY CALL THIS TOLL-FREE NUMBER NOW, AND LET THE MUTANT PROFESSIONALS HANDLE IT FROM THERE! VISA AND MASTERCARD ARE ACCEPTED! *YOU DON'T HAVE TO LIVE IN FEAR ANYMORE!* =CLICK=

1-800-555-937

PLEASE UNDERSTAND THAT THE PROFIT MOTIVE IS THERE SIMPLY AS A DETERRENT. WE DON'T AROUSE SUSPICIONS OF OUR *TRUE* INTENTIONS. CHARMINGLY IRONIC, THOUGH, DON'T YOU THINK?

HODGE, HOW LONG BEFORE THESE SPOTS BEGIN TO AIR?

WELL, ACTUALLY, MR. SUMMERS, THEY HAVE ALREADY BEEN AIRING FOR SEVERAL DAYS NOW!

WHAT?!!

I HATE TO WASTE ANY TIME! SHALL WE BEGIN BRIEFING ON OPERATIONS, GENTLEMEN?

MEANWHILE, AT THE NAVAL SECURITY FACILITY IN SAN DIEGO, RUSTY COLLINS BEGINS ANOTHER DAY OF INCARCERATION IN SOLITARY CONFINEMENT...

SAN DIEGO NAVAL MAXIMUM SECURITY FACILITY

91

BUT TODAY, HE'S ABOUT TO RECEIVE AN UNEXPECTED VISITOR...

HIYA, BOYS! I HEAR DA MUTIE AIN'T ALLOWED NO CALLERS!

I DON'T SEE ANYONE! HOW ABOUT YOU, JACK?

NOT A SOUL!

HEY, MUTIE! WHERE YA HIDIN', SCUM-BALL?

DA WORD IS THEY'RE GONNA MOVE YA TA SOME MEDICAL CENTER FOR TESTS, MUTIE! DEY THINK DAT YA MIGHT NOT O' INTENTIONALLY HURT EMMA! I KNOW BETTER, FREAK!

CH-CHIEF...!

DA WAY I GOT IT FIGURED, DEY DON'T CARE WHAT SHAPE YER IN WHEN DEY TEST YA, MUTIE!

CH-CHIEF-- I-I'M SORRY! I-I DIDN'T MEAN TO--

SHUDDUP, FREAK! I DECIDED DAT DEY CAN DO AN AUTOPSY ON YA AS EASY AS ANYTHIN' ELSE--SO I CAME TA SEE WHAT I COULD DO 'BOUT HELPIN' 'EM OUT, RUSTY!

GUARDS! GUARDS!

SAVE YER BREATH! YA AIN'T GOT TOO MANY LEFT AS IT IS! HA, HA, HA!

CLICK

N-NO! NOT AGAIN! PLEASE...!

NOOOOO!

ARRGH! MY HAND!

GET AWAY CHIEF! IT'S OUTTA CONTROL! IT'S--

SHRAK-A-BOOM!

I-I'VE GOT TO GET AWAY-- FAR AWAY! I-I'M NOT GOING TO LET THEM CUT ME UP!

≡KOFF≡ LOUSY... ≡CHOKE≡ MUTIE... SCUM...

NO! THEY'RE SOUNDING THE BASE ALARMS! THEY'RE ALL AFTER ME! PLEASE--

--LEAVE ME ALONE! STAY BACK! I CAN'T CONTROL IT!!

WITHIN THREE MINUTES, HALF THE BASE IS A SMOLDERING RUIN... AND RUSTY IS ON THE LOOSE!

AND A FEW HOURS LATER, AT A LOCAL PUB...

IF DEY CAPTURE DA KID, HE'S GONNA SPILL DA BEANS ABOUT WHAT I TRIED TA DO! I GOTTA THINK O' SOMETHIN'!

HEY, FISH! HOWZIT GOIN'? PULL UP A SEAT!

HEY, HAVE YA SEEN DIS AD ON DA TUBE? MAYBE THEY COULD HANDLE THAT KID O' YOURS?

ELMO, D'YA THINK DOSE GUYS ARE FER REAL?

X-FACTOR
NO NEED TO BE FEARFUL ANY LONGER!
MEN

AS FAR AS I KNOW! DERE ON DA T.V., AIN'T DEY? I--

GIMME SOME CHANGE, ELMO! I WANNA MAKE A CALL--

CALL TODAY 1(800)555-4387

93

AN HOUR LATER, BACK IN N.Y.C.

SCOTT? WHAT ARE YOU DOING? DIDN'T YOU HEAR? WE'VE GOT AN **ASSIGNMENT!** LET'S GO!

THIS WHOLE THING IS LUDICROUS, JEAN. IT'S NOT GOING TO WORK!

SCOTT-- YOU **HAVE** TO BELIEVE IT WILL! THE GROUP IS DEPENDING ON YOU!

THAT ONLY MAKES IT WORSE!

LOOK-- IF NOT FOR ANYTHING ELSE, DO IT BECAUSE I WANT YOU TO BE **WITH** ME, OKAY?

THAT'S THE ONLY REASON I'M STILL HERE, JEAN!

THEN-- YOU'RE COMING?

I--I GUESS...

I'LL HAVE TO BE AROUND AT LEAST LONG ENOUGH TO TELL YOU ABOUT MADELYNE!

A SHORT TIME LATER, AT LA GUARDIA INTERNATIONAL AIRPORT...

HOLY--! WOULD YOU TAKE A LOOK AT THAT!?

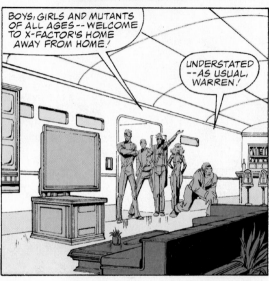

BOYS, GIRLS AND MUTANTS OF ALL AGES -- WELCOME TO X-FACTOR'S HOME AWAY FROM HOME!

UNDERSTATED --AS USUAL, WARREN!

FIVE HOURS LATER, THE AIRCRAFT TOUCHES DOWN IN SAN DIEGO... AND...

I WISH WE DIDN'T HAVE TO LEAVE HANK AND WARREN BEHIND, JEANIE!

I KNOW, BOBBY, BUT FACE IT-- THEY COULDN'T EXACTLY PASS FOR HUMAN, COULD THEY?

THAT'S RIGHT! IF WE NEED TO GO INTO ACTION AS THE ORIGINAL **X-MEN** NO ONE MUST MAKE A CONNECTION BETWEEN THEM AND **X-FACTOR!**

IN THE AIRPORT LOUNGE--

THAT MUST BE HIM-- THE NAVY GUY OVER THERE!

C.P.O. FISHER?

UH... YEAH?

YOU CALLED FOR US.

SO--DIS STINKIN' MUTIE BURNS MY GIRLFRIEND REALLY BAD AN' THEN BLOWS UP HALF DA BASE! I CALLED YA 'CAUSE I...ER... DON'T THINK DA MILITARY POLICE'RE GONNA BE ABLE TA STOP 'IM! SO FAR, DA LITTLE FREAK'S HELD DEM OFF REAL GOOD! ARE YA GONNA USE MUTIE DISINTEGRATORS OR SOMETHIN'?

WE HAVE OUR METHODS, CHIEF FISHER.

WHAT A SLIME-BALL!

JUST THE FACTS NOW, CHIEF! WHERE HAS THE PURSUIT LED THE MILITARY?

OUTSIDE O'TOWN--ABOUT TEN MILES INTA DA HILL AREA! WORD IS, HE'S STILL ON DA LOOSE!

DON'T WORRY-- WE'LL GET HIM-- THAT'S WHAT YOU HIRED X-FACTOR FOR.

A SHORT TIME LATER, IN THE COUNTRYSIDE AROUND SAN DIEGO...

BLUE LEADER-- THIS IS MOTHER BIRD! COVERAGE ON TARGET --ORDERS ARE TO SHOOT TO KILL, IF NECESSARY!

NOOOO! ARE YOU CRAZY?! I DON'T WANT TO HURT YOU! PLEASE!

I'M NOT GOING TO LET YOU HURT ME! IF I'VE GOT TO, I'LL--

LOOK OUT! JUMP!

SHRAKKK

WH-WHAT WAS THAT?!

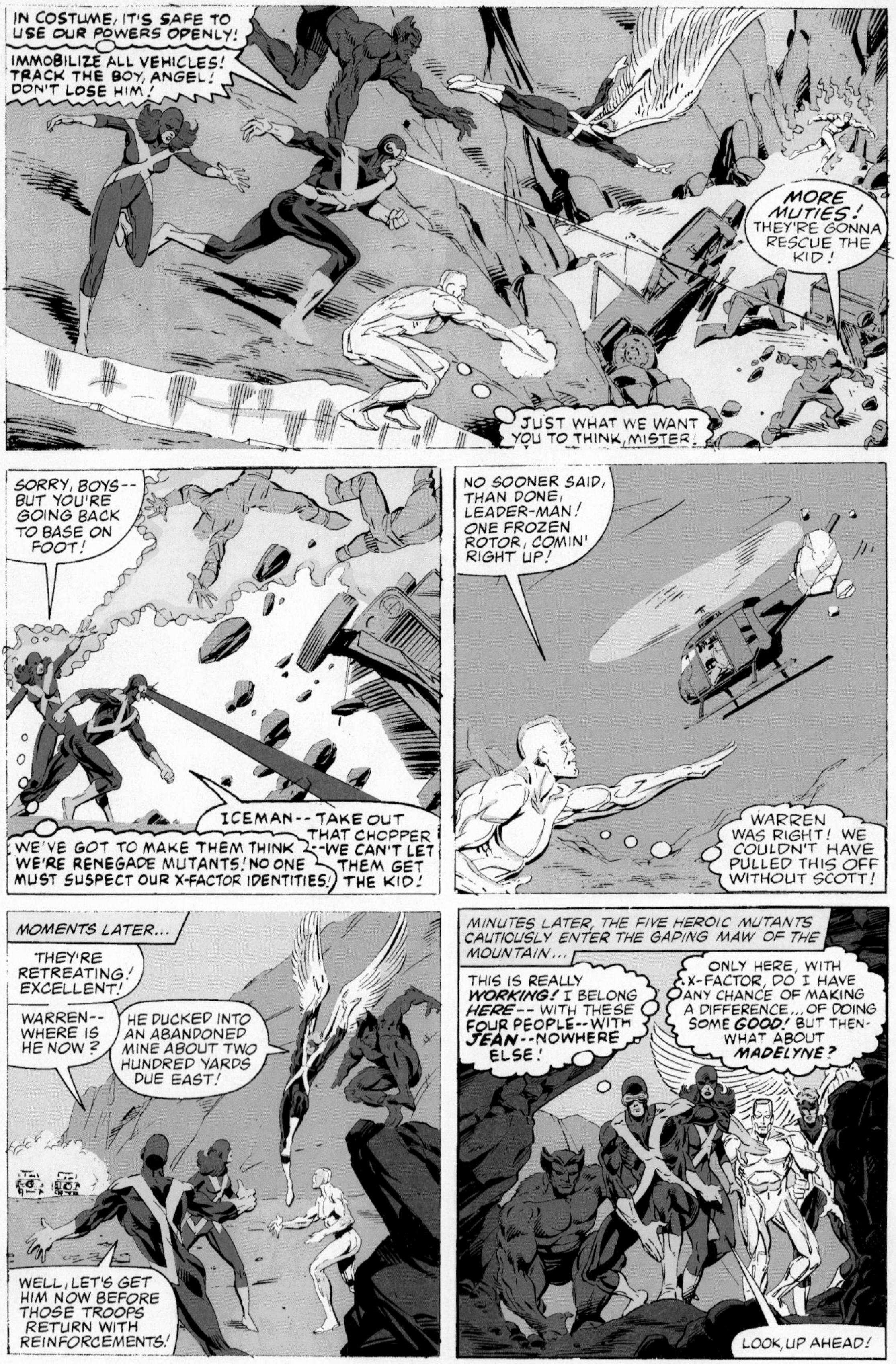

IN COSTUME, IT'S SAFE TO USE OUR POWERS OPENLY!
IMMOBILIZE ALL VEHICLES! TRACK THE BOY, ANGEL! DON'T LOSE HIM!
MORE MUTIES! THEY'RE GONNA RESCUE THE KID!
JUST WHAT WE WANT YOU TO THINK, MISTER!
SORRY, BOYS-- BUT YOU'RE GOING BACK TO BASE ON FOOT!
ICEMAN-- TAKE OUT THAT CHOPPER --WE CAN'T LET THEM GET THE KID!
WE'VE GOT TO MAKE THEM THINK WE'RE RENEGADE MUTANTS! NO ONE MUST SUSPECT OUR X-FACTOR IDENTITIES!
NO SOONER SAID, THAN DONE, LEADER-MAN! ONE FROZEN ROTOR, COMIN' RIGHT UP!
WARREN WAS RIGHT! WE COULDN'T HAVE PULLED THIS OFF WITHOUT SCOTT!
MOMENTS LATER...
THEY'RE RETREATING! EXCELLENT!
WARREN-- WHERE IS HE NOW?
HE DUCKED INTO AN ABANDONED MINE ABOUT TWO HUNDRED YARDS DUE EAST!
WELL, LET'S GET HIM NOW BEFORE THOSE TROOPS RETURN WITH REINFORCEMENTS!
MINUTES LATER, THE FIVE HEROIC MUTANTS CAUTIOUSLY ENTER THE GAPING MAW OF THE MOUNTAIN...
THIS IS REALLY WORKING! I BELONG HERE-- WITH THESE FOUR PEOPLE--WITH JEAN--NOWHERE ELSE!
ONLY HERE, WITH X-FACTOR, DO I HAVE ANY CHANCE OF MAKING A DIFFERENCE... OF DOING SOME GOOD! BUT THEN-WHAT ABOUT MADELYNE?
LOOK, UP AHEAD!

THAT LIGHT-- I-IT'S SO EERIE!

IT HAS TO BE HIM!

COME ON OUT, SON! WE WANT TO HELP YOU!

NO! GO AWAY! NO ONE CAN... HELP ME! P-PLEASE... I DON'T... WANT TO... HURT... YOU!

THE GROUP REACHES THE SOURCE OF THE LIGHT, ONLY TO BE FROZEN IN THEIR TRACKS...

...BY THE BIZARRE SCENE BEFORE THEM.

GOOD HEAVENS--!

HE APPEARS AS A TORMENTED SOUL IN THE DEPTHS OF HADES-- FLAMES DANCING AROUND HIM IN A PYRO-TECHNIC BALLET THAT ECHOES HIS RAGE...

I DON'T KNOW WHO YOU ARE BUT YOU AIN'T GONNA USE ME AS NO GUINEA PIG!

SON--LOOK! YOU DON'T UNDERSTAND! WE'RE HERE TO--

NO! NO MORE LIES! YOU'RE NOT TAKING ME BACK! BEFORE THAT HAPPENS I'LL--

--BURN YOU ALL!!

HE'S SCARED! OBVIOUSLY NOT IN CONTROL!

GOOD! THAT MEANS HE'S NOT THE NEXT *MAGNETO*!

THAT SHOULD MAKE THIS EASIER... WE'VE GOT TO GET HIM OUT OF HERE AND BACK TO HOME-BASE. MAYBE THERE WE'LL BE ABLE TO GAIN HIS *TRUST*!

BUT TO DO THAT WE'VE GOT TO TAKE HIM OUT NOW! POSITIONS EVERYONE...

ATTACK!

KEEP HIM OFF BALANCE... DON'T LET HIM PUT HIS POWERS INTO PLAY!

CYCLOPS--THIS CAVERN CAN'T TAKE THE STRESS OF THIS KIND OF HEAT FOR LONG!

JUST THEN, AS IF TO PUNCTUATE THE BEAST'S WORDS, THE CEILING STARTS TO GIVE WAY--AND THE ANGEL IS ONLY MOMENTS FROM DEATH, WHEN...

DON'T WORRY, MY WINGED COMPATRIOT--I'VE GOT YOU! ICEMAN--!

SAY NO MORE! I GOT HIM! NICE TEAMWORK, EH?

I'M WARNING YOU-- STAY BACK--I'LL BRING THIS WHOLE PLACE DOWN! I MEAN IT!

SORRY, RUSTY-- BUT YOU'RE COMING WITH US, *FOR YOUR OWN GOOD*!

98

I'D RATHER DIE!!

WOOROOOSH!

CYKE--THE CAVE'S COLLAPSING!

NO TIME TO LOSE--MANEUVER TWELVE--*NOW!*

WITH LIGHTNING SPEED, ANGEL AND CYCLOPS STRIKE, RENDERING THE BOY HELPLESS...

IT'S TOO LATE, SCOTT --THE MINE IS *CAVING IN!*

THE THUNDEROUS CASCADE OF ROCK IS FOLLOWED BY--

--AN OMINOUS SILENCE!

BUT...

S-SCOTT! PLEASE H-HURRY! I-I CAN'T HOLD THIS WEIGHT FOR L-LONG! OH--

HANG ON, JEAN!

JEAN--ALL MY FRIENDS --WOULD BE DEAD BY NOW IF I HADN'T COME WITH THEM! IF I WASN'T HERE... I WOULD HAVE LOST HER AGAIN! AND THE BOY, RUSTY, WOULD HAVE DIED WITHOUT A CHANCE FOR A DECENT LIFE!

OF THE GROUP, ONLY I HAVE THE POWER TO SAVE US NOW! FINALLY, I REALIZE WHAT I NEED TO DO AND--

--WE *WILL* BE FREE!!

SHRAKK

KRAK-KA-KA-THOOM

SECONDS LATER, AS THE DUST CLEARS...

BOY! DID THAT FEEL *GOOD*! SCOTT, YOU WERE *GREAT*--WE WERE *ALL* GREAT!

HE'S RIGHT! AND WE DID JUST WHAT WE SET OUT TO DO --JUST LIKE THE OLD DAYS!

NOT QUITE, HANK! UNLIKE OLD TIMES, YOU AND WARREN HAVE TO HIDE OUT! WE CAN'T AFFORD TO BE SEEN TOGETHER!

WE AREN'T A TOTAL SUCCESS YET. YOU'VE GOT THE KID ALL WRAPPED UP NICE AND TIDY, IN THIS LITTLE ASBESTOS BAG! *NOW WHAT?*

FIRST, BOBBY, JEAN AND I CHANGE BACK INTO X-FACTOR GEAR! IT'S IMPORTANT THAT WE'RE SPOTTED ON THE SCENE CAPTURING A DANGEROUS MUTANT! THEN WE CONTACT FISHER AND CLOSE THIS CASE--HOPEFULLY WITHOUT FURTHER COMPLICATIONS!

A FEW HOURS LATER, INSIDE THE X-FACTOR AIRCRAFT...

GAWD--DEY ACTUALLY *CAUGHT 'IM!*

MISSION ACCOMPLISHED, CHIEF! ONE CAPTIVE MUTANT--COURTESY OF X-FACTOR, INC.!

I SUPPOSE YOU'LL WANT US TO TURN HIM OVER TO THE NAVAL AUTHORITIES?

AH...ER...WELL, WHY DON'T YOU GUYS TAKE 'IM AND C-CONDUCT YER TESTS ON 'IM OR SOMETHIN'?

WHATEVER YOU SAY, CHIEF. BUT THERE IS STILL ONE OTHER ITEM WE HAVE TO TAKE CARE OF.

100

WHAT DO YA MEAN?

THERE *IS* THE SMALL MATTER OF THE BILL FOR SERVICES RENDERED!

WHA...?!! *42,000 DOLLARS!!!* N-NO FREAKIN' WAY! DAT'S TWO YEAR'S PAY!!

WELL--I SUPPOSE WE COULD PUT THE MUTANT BACK WHERE WE FOUND HIM. THE AUTHORITIES WOULD HAVE HAD HIM SOON ANY--

ER...N-NO... *NO!* DIS LOOKS CORRECT TA ME! M-MY MISTAKE!

HA, HA, HA! I COULD LEARN TO LIKE THIS! WE GET WHAT WE WANT AND TAKE THE MUTANT-HATERS TO THE CLEANERS AT THE SAME TIME! HA-HA-HA!!

"CHARMINGLY IRONIC" AT THAT, EH? HA, HA, HA!

A SHORT TIME LATER, AS THE X-FACTOR JET FLIES EASTWARD...

EASY, RUSTY! WE CAN SAFELY GET YOU OUT OF THAT NOW!

WHA...? WHERE AM I?!

REST EASY, SON! YOU'RE AMONG FRIENDS... FINALLY!

HERE'S SOMETHING TO PUT ON, RUSTY!

YOU'RE THE PEOPLE IN THE CAVE, AIN'T YOU? YOU-- YOU *SAVED ME!?* WHY? AIN'T YOU ASCARED OF ME TOO?

NO, SON...WE KNOW WHAT YOU'VE BEEN GOING THROUGH-- EACH ONE OF US WENT THROUGH THE SAME THING WHEN WE WERE YOUR AGE.

I DIDN'T KNOW *WHAT* WAS HAPPENING.

WELL, FRIEND, THAT'S WHAT WE'RE HERE FOR. WE HAD HELP AND GUIDANCE THEN--AND IF YOU'D ALLOW US, WE'D LIKE TO HELP *YOU!*

TH-THANK YOU! BUT...IF YOU'RE LIKE ME, HOW DID YOU GET PAST ALL THOSE REGULAR PEOPLE TO GET TO ME?

AFTER A BRIEF DESCRIPTION OF THE BASIC X-FACTOR SERVICE AND...

HAR! THAT'S A REAL CRAZY IDEA! AND YOU MEAN TO SAY THAT THE CHIEF SWALLOWED THAT LOAD OF--

HOOK, LINE, *AND* SINKER!

IT'S GOING TO WORK, ISN'T IT, WARREN?

YOU BET, JEAN! X-FACTOR IS HERE TO STAY!

THAT SAME NIGHT, IN ANCHORAGE, ALASKA...

THREE THIRTY, A.M....

X-FACTOR MUTANT INVESTIGATIONS AND SOLUTIONS!

NEXT ISSUE: "BRING ME THE HEAD OF HANK McCOY!"

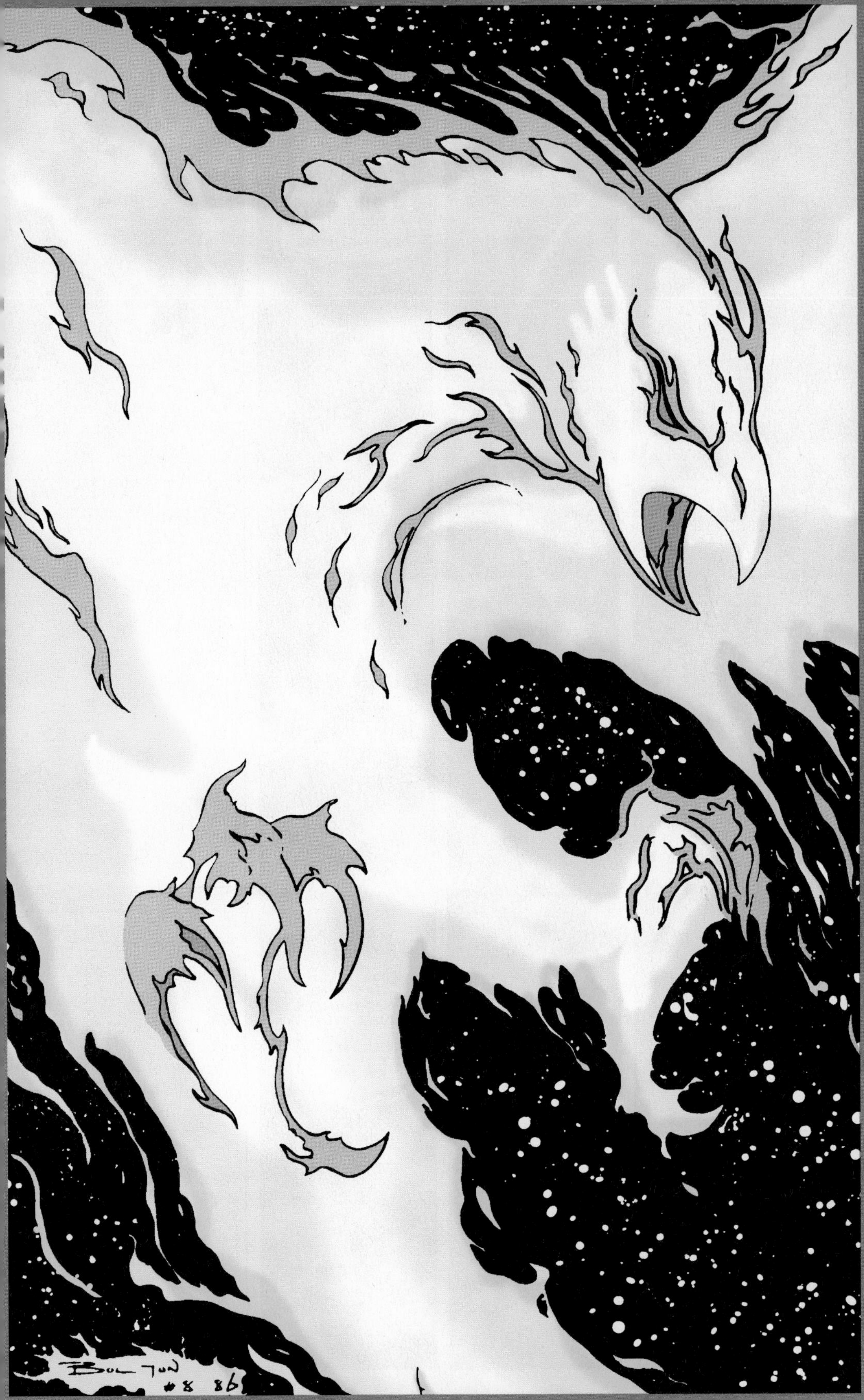
BOLTON
#8 86

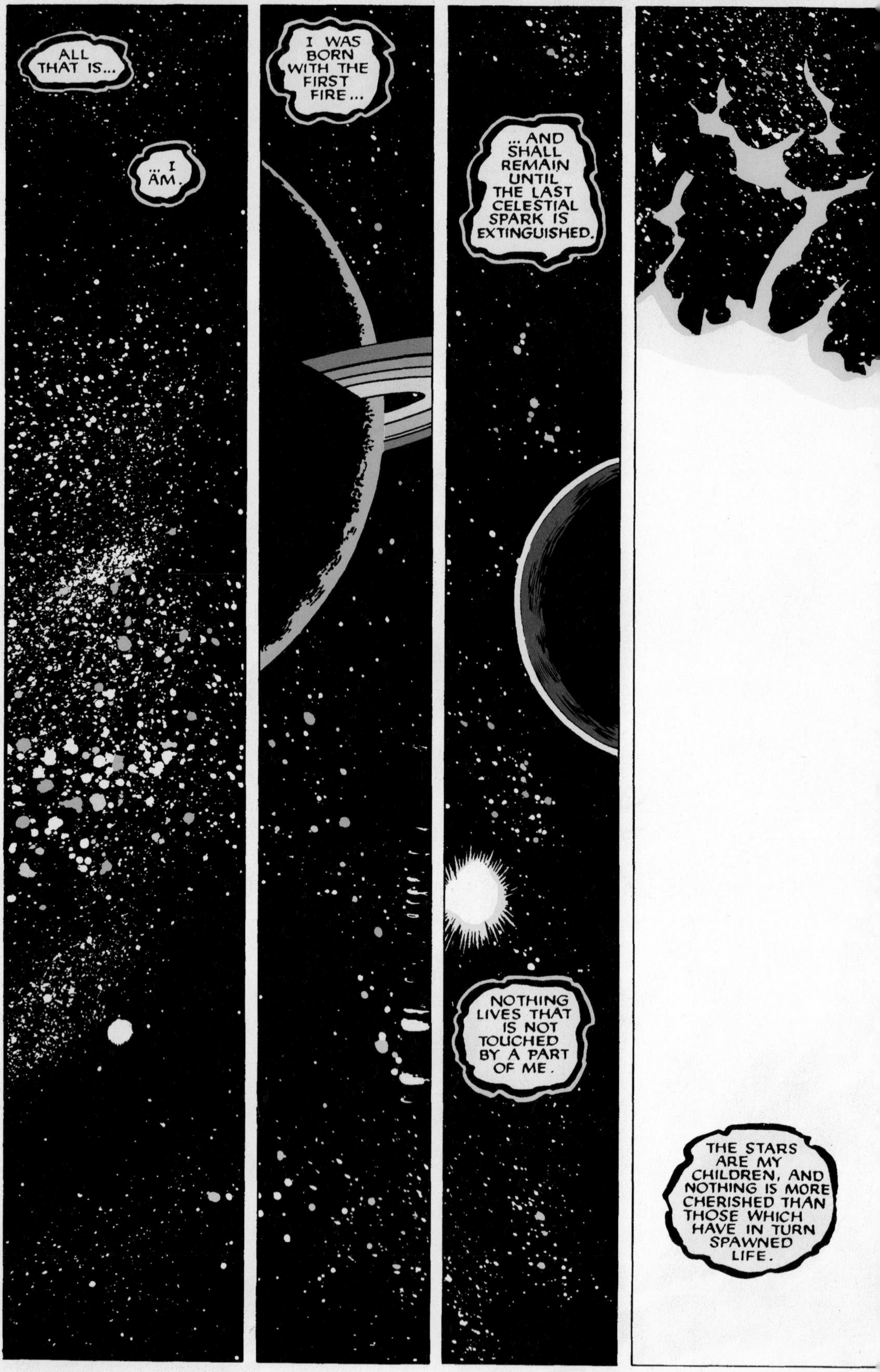
ALL THAT IS...
... I AM.
I WAS BORN WITH THE FIRST FIRE...
... AND SHALL REMAIN UNTIL THE LAST CELESTIAL SPARK IS EXTINGUISHED.
NOTHING LIVES THAT IS NOT TOUCHED BY A PART OF ME.
THE STARS ARE MY CHILDREN, AND NOTHING IS MORE CHERISHED THAN THOSE WHICH HAVE IN TURN SPAWNED LIFE.

HIGH ABOVE THE THIRD ORB, CALLED THE *EARTH*...

...A CONSTRUCT TUMBLES THROUGH THE DARK...

...WHILE ANOTHER SMALLER VEHICLE PLUNGES RECKLESSLY TOWARDS ITS HOMEWORLD, FLEEING THE WILD ENERGIES OF A SOLAR FLARE SURGING INVISIBLY OUTWARDS FROM THE SUN.

THERE ARE NOBLE SOULS WITHIN. AND DOOMED, AS WELL.

AMONG THEM, THE REASON FOR MY PRESENCE.

JEAN!

SCOTT, *NO!* IF YOU OPEN THE LIFE-CELL, YOU'LL *KILL US ALL!*

LET ME GO, BLAST YOU!

I CAN'T STAY HERE, SAFE IN THE CARGO BAY...

...WHILE SHE'S ALONE UP THERE ON THE FLIGHT DECK!

LET ME GO TO HER, NIGHTCRAWLER-- HELP HER-- BEFORE IT'S *TOO LATE!*

IT'S *ALREADY* TOO LATE, MY FRIEND!

SHE KNOWS THAT, YOU MUST ACCEPT IT!

PLEASE, KURT-- I *BEG* YOU!

CYCLOPS, WOULD YOU HAVE HER SACRIFICE BE IN VAIN?!

PLEASE...

...I *LOVE* HER...

...I DON'T WANT HER TO *DIE!*

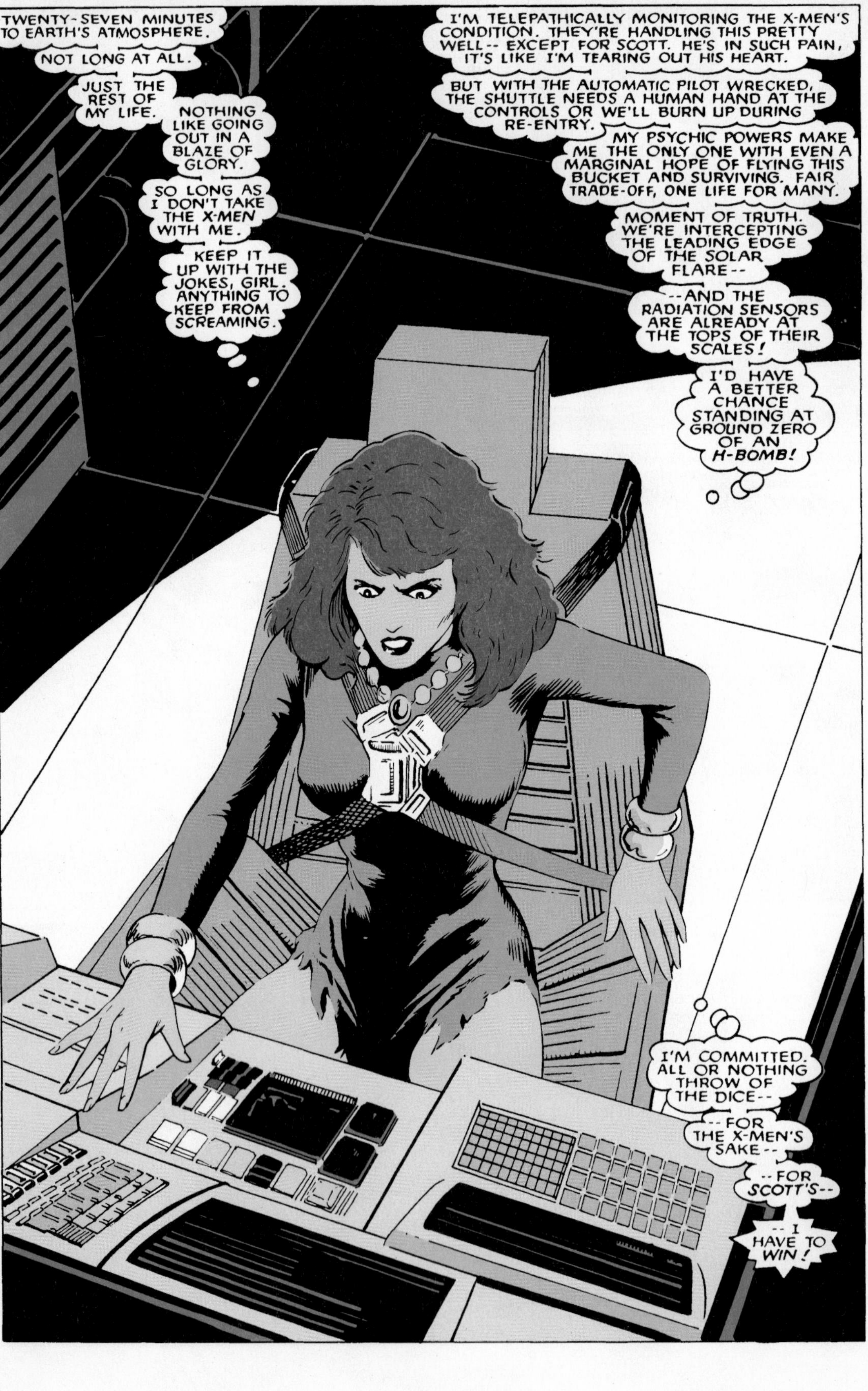
TWENTY-SEVEN MINUTES TO EARTH'S ATMOSPHERE.
NOT LONG AT ALL.
JUST THE REST OF MY LIFE.
NOTHING LIKE GOING OUT IN A BLAZE OF GLORY.
SO LONG AS I DON'T TAKE THE X-MEN WITH ME.
KEEP IT UP WITH THE JOKES, GIRL. ANYTHING TO KEEP FROM SCREAMING.
I'M TELEPATHICALLY MONITORING THE X-MEN'S CONDITION. THEY'RE HANDLING THIS PRETTY WELL -- EXCEPT FOR SCOTT. HE'S IN SUCH PAIN, IT'S LIKE I'M TEARING OUT HIS HEART.
BUT WITH THE AUTOMATIC PILOT WRECKED, THE SHUTTLE NEEDS A HUMAN HAND AT THE CONTROLS OR WE'LL BURN UP DURING RE-ENTRY.
MY PSYCHIC POWERS MAKE ME THE ONLY ONE WITH EVEN A MARGINAL HOPE OF FLYING THIS BUCKET AND SURVIVING. FAIR TRADE-OFF, ONE LIFE FOR MANY.
MOMENT OF TRUTH. WE'RE INTERCEPTING THE LEADING EDGE OF THE SOLAR FLARE--
--AND THE RADIATION SENSORS ARE ALREADY AT THE TOPS OF THEIR SCALES!
I'D HAVE A BETTER CHANCE STANDING AT GROUND ZERO OF AN H-BOMB!
I'M COMMITTED. ALL OR NOTHING THROW OF THE DICE--
--FOR THE X-MEN'S SAKE--
--FOR SCOTT'S--
--I HAVE TO WIN!

THE CHILD'S WILL FAR OUTSTRIPS HER STRENGTH.

SHE KNOWS THIS--

-- AND THE BEGINNINGS OF *FEAR* AS WELL.

TWENTY MINUTES MORE, AT LEAST.

I'VE NEVER SEEN RAD-COUNTS SO HIGH. FOR WHAT IT'S WORTH, OUTSIDE OF THIS SHIELDED COMPARTMENT, ANY OF THE REST OF US WOULD BE DEAD IN SECONDS.

JEAN GREY'S OUR ONLY HOPE, X-MEN--

"--AND A SLIM ONE, AT BEST. IT'S A MIRACLE SHE'S LASTED THIS LONG!"

JUST STUBBORN, I GUESS, Dr. CORBEAU-- OLD FAMILY TRAIT--

-- BUT "THANKS" FOR THE VOTE OF CONFIDENCE.

SOME DAYS IT JUST DOESN'T PAY TO BE ABLE TO READ MINDS.

THIS IS BAD-- I COUNTED ON THE TELEKINETIC SIDE OF MY POWERS TO SCREEN OUT THE BULK OF THE RADIATION, BUT THE PRESSURE'S *TOO GREAT!*

DEAR LORD, HEAR MY PRAYER--

-- AND *HELP ME!*

THE FLARE-- MY PSI-SHIELDS... COLLAPSING-- IT *HURTS!*

SCOTT!

FLESH WITHERS UNDER THE SAVAGE ONSLAUGHT...

...YET HER SPIRIT SOARS-- HIGHER, MORE FIERCELY DEFIANT, THAN EVER!

SO QUICK. SO BRUTAL.

CAN BARELY SEE-- ULTRA-VIOLET OCCLUDING MY EYES WITH CATARACTS.

BLEEDING-- INSIDE AND OUT-- MASSIVE HEMOR-RHAGING AS CELLULAR BONDS DISSOLVE. LOSING MY HAIR, TOO. WISH THAT WAS THE WORST OF IT.

LUCKY I'M WEIGHTLESS. HEART WOULD BURST UNDER THE STRAIN OF GRAVITY, MY BONES WOULD CRUMBLE TO POWDER.

THIS ISN'T FAIR--

--IT ISN'T RIGHT--

--NOT WHEN I'VE FOUGHT SO HARD--

--!?!

LIGHT-- BEHIND ME--

--AN EXPLOSION?! ARE WE ON FIRE?!!

DON'T BE FOOLISH.

CAN'T BE ANYTHING I CAN SEE...

...BECAUSE I'M BLIND.

WHAT, THEN?

HALLUCINATION??

PAIN-- --IT'S GONE!

NO! NO! NO!

I WON'T DIE, I WON'T GIVE UP-- NOT WHILE SO MUCH STILL DEPENDS ON ME!

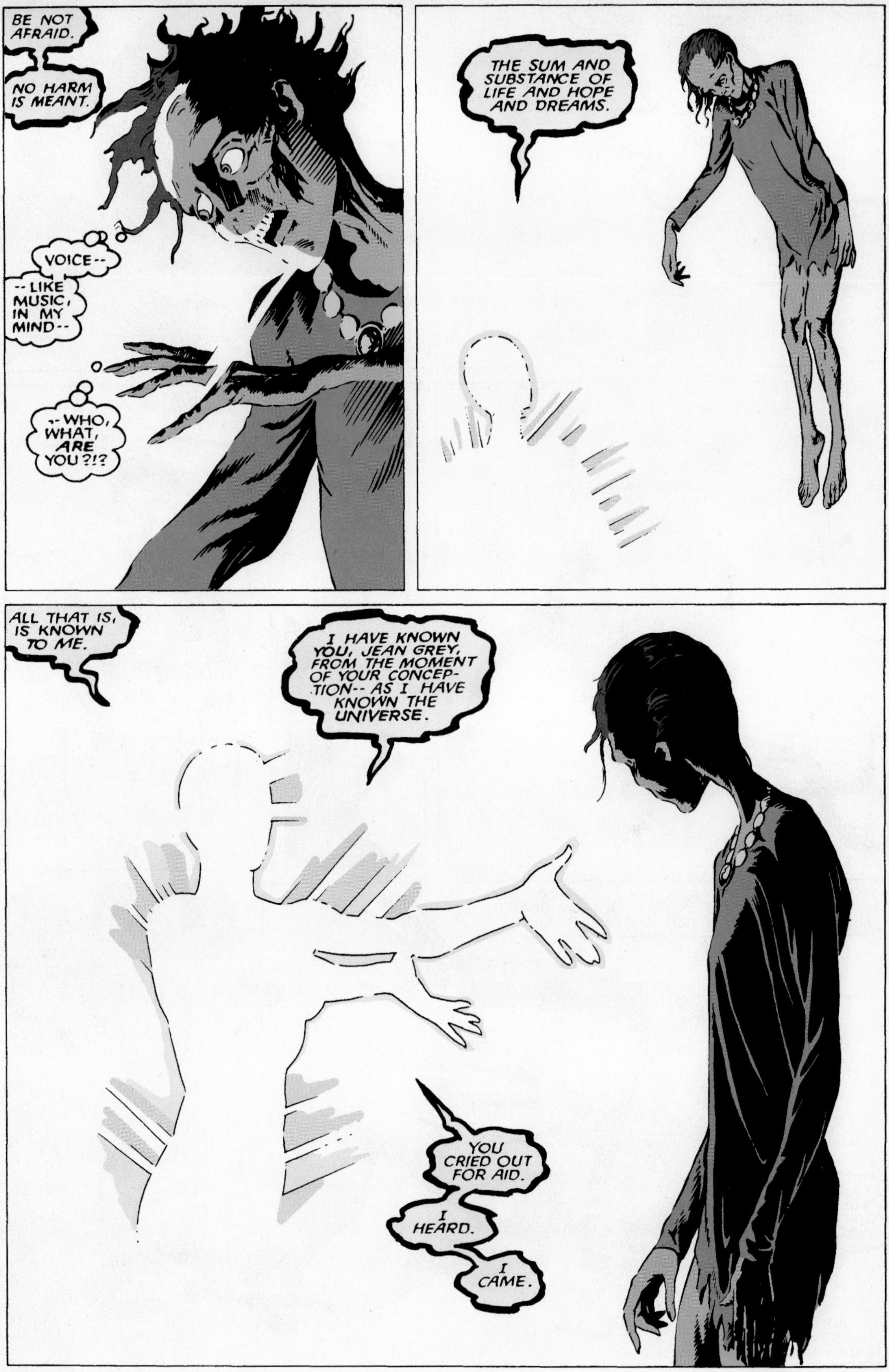
BE NOT AFRAID.
NO HARM IS MEANT.
VOICE--
--LIKE MUSIC, IN MY MIND--
--WHO, WHAT, ARE YOU?!?
THE SUM AND SUBSTANCE OF LIFE AND HOPE AND DREAMS.
ALL THAT IS, IS KNOWN TO ME.
I HAVE KNOWN YOU, JEAN GREY, FROM THE MOMENT OF YOUR CONCEPTION-- AS I HAVE KNOWN THE UNIVERSE.
YOU CRIED OUT FOR AID.
I HEARD.
I CAME.

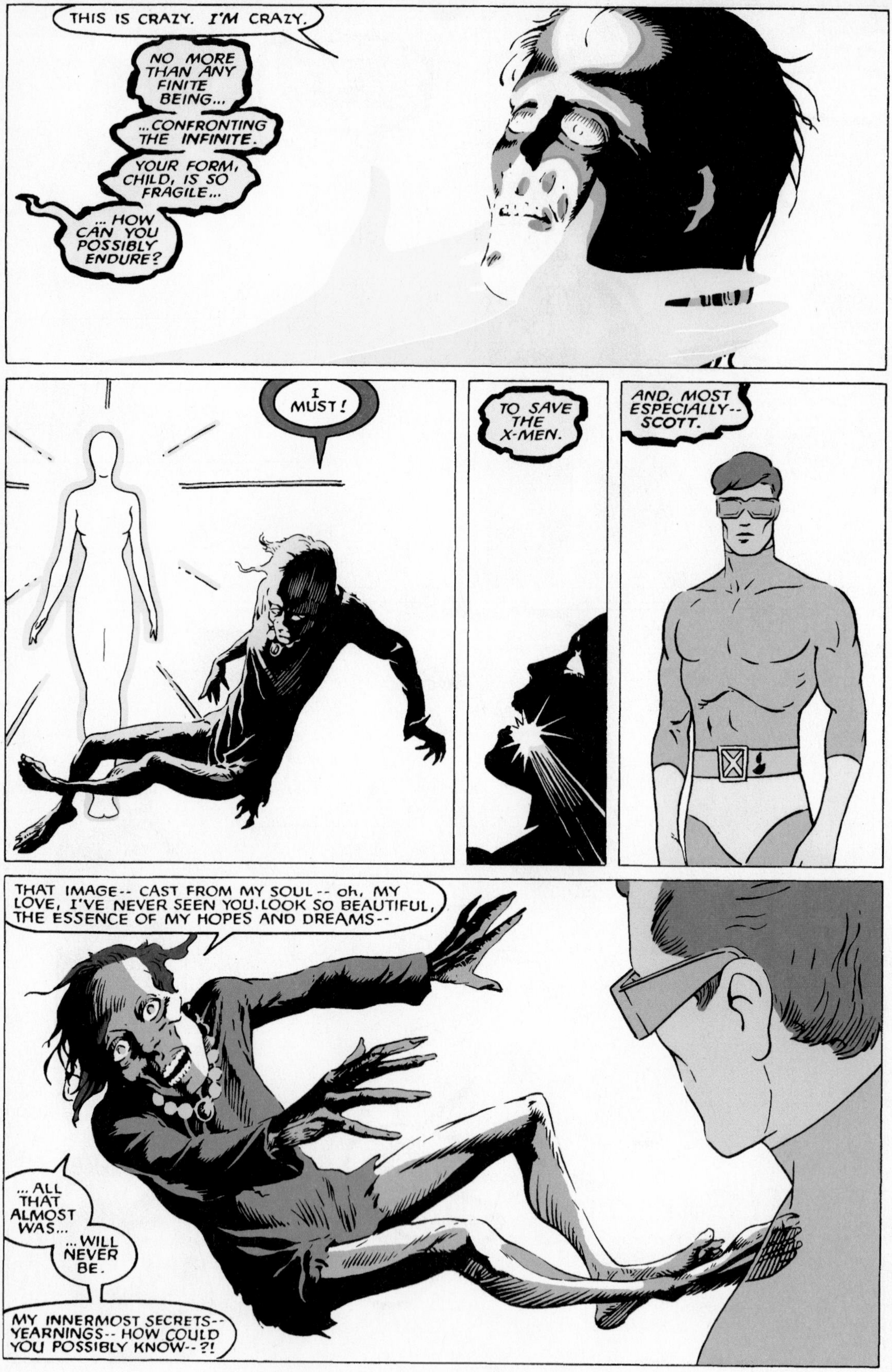
THIS IS CRAZY. I'M CRAZY.
NO MORE THAN ANY FINITE BEING...
...CONFRONTING THE INFINITE.
YOUR FORM, CHILD, IS SO FRAGILE...
...HOW CAN YOU POSSIBLY ENDURE?
I MUST!
TO SAVE THE X-MEN.
AND, MOST ESPECIALLY-- SCOTT.
THAT IMAGE-- CAST FROM MY SOUL-- oh, MY LOVE, I'VE NEVER SEEN YOU LOOK SO BEAUTIFUL, THE ESSENCE OF MY HOPES AND DREAMS--
...ALL THAT ALMOST WAS...
...WILL NEVER BE.
MY INNERMOST SECRETS-- YEARNINGS-- HOW COULD YOU POSSIBLY KNOW--?!

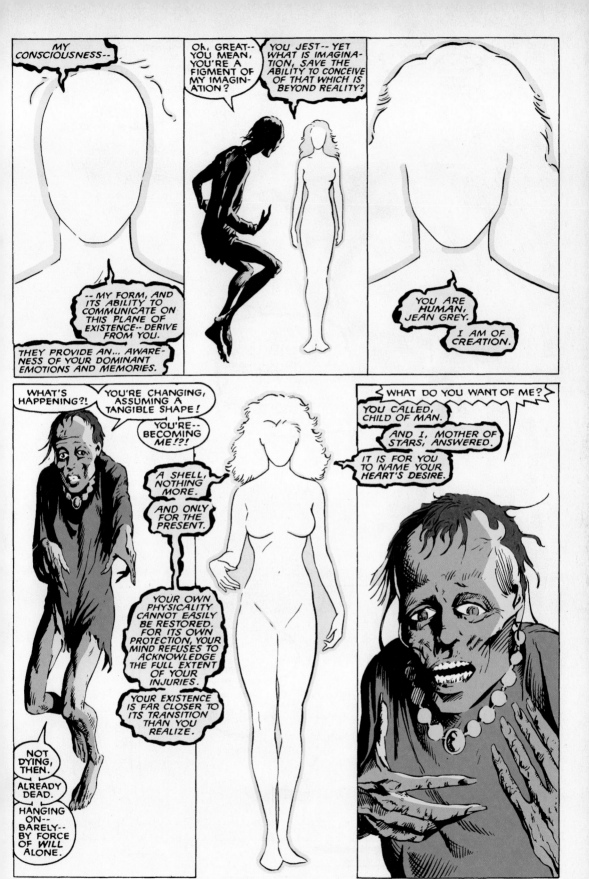

MY CONSCIOUSNESS--

OH, GREAT-- YOU MEAN, YOU'RE A FIGMENT OF MY IMAGINATION?

YOU JEST-- YET WHAT IS IMAGINATION, SAVE THE ABILITY TO CONCEIVE OF THAT WHICH IS BEYOND REALITY?

-- MY FORM, AND ITS ABILITY TO COMMUNICATE ON THIS PLANE OF EXISTENCE-- DERIVE FROM YOU.

THEY PROVIDE AN... AWARENESS OF YOUR DOMINANT EMOTIONS AND MEMORIES.

YOU ARE HUMAN, JEAN GREY.

I AM OF CREATION.

WHAT'S HAPPENING?!

YOU'RE CHANGING, ASSUMING A TANGIBLE SHAPE!

YOU'RE-- BECOMING ME!?!

A SHELL, NOTHING MORE.

AND ONLY FOR THE PRESENT.

YOUR OWN PHYSICALITY CANNOT EASILY BE RESTORED. FOR ITS OWN PROTECTION, YOUR MIND REFUSES TO ACKNOWLEDGE THE FULL EXTENT OF YOUR INJURIES.

YOUR EXISTENCE IS FAR CLOSER TO ITS TRANSITION THAN YOU REALIZE.

NOT DYING, THEN.

ALREADY DEAD.

HANGING ON-- BARELY-- BY FORCE OF WILL ALONE.

WHAT DO YOU WANT OF ME?

YOU CALLED, CHILD OF MAN.

AND I, MOTHER OF STARS, ANSWERED.

IT IS FOR YOU TO NAME YOUR HEART'S DESIRE.

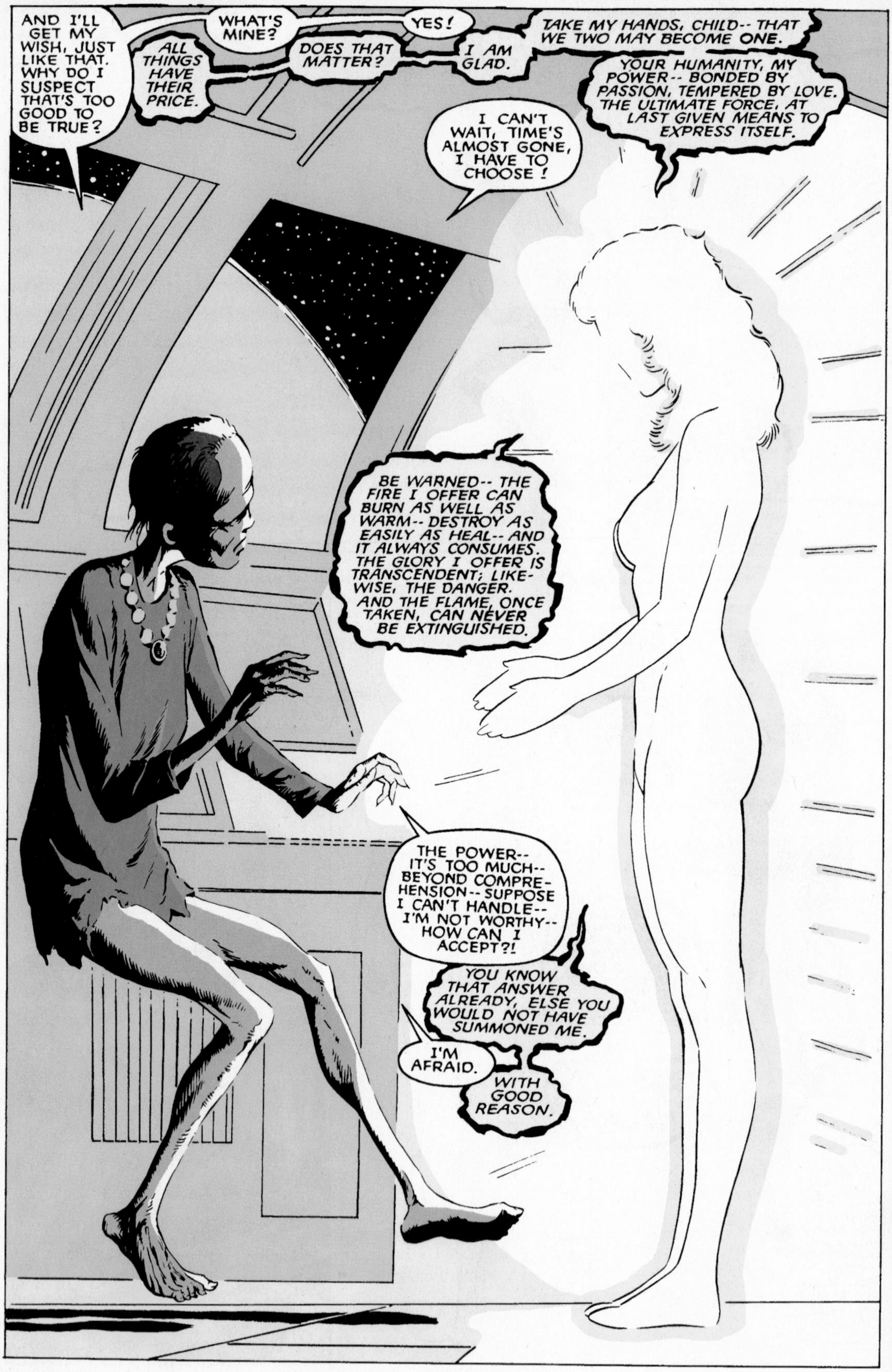
AND I'LL GET MY WISH, JUST LIKE THAT. WHY DO I SUSPECT THAT'S TOO GOOD TO BE TRUE?
ALL THINGS HAVE THEIR PRICE.
WHAT'S MINE?
DOES THAT MATTER?
YES!
I AM GLAD.
TAKE MY HANDS, CHILD-- THAT WE TWO MAY BECOME ONE.
YOUR HUMANITY, MY POWER-- BONDED BY PASSION, TEMPERED BY LOVE. THE ULTIMATE FORCE, AT LAST GIVEN MEANS TO EXPRESS ITSELF.
I CAN'T WAIT, TIME'S ALMOST GONE, I HAVE TO CHOOSE!
BE WARNED-- THE FIRE I OFFER CAN BURN AS WELL AS WARM-- DESTROY AS EASILY AS HEAL-- AND IT ALWAYS CONSUMES. THE GLORY I OFFER IS TRANSCENDENT; LIKEWISE, THE DANGER. AND THE FLAME, ONCE TAKEN, CAN NEVER BE EXTINGUISHED.
THE POWER-- IT'S TOO MUCH-- BEYOND COMPREHENSION-- SUPPOSE I CAN'T HANDLE-- I'M NOT WORTHY-- HOW CAN I ACCEPT?!
YOU KNOW THAT ANSWER ALREADY, ELSE YOU WOULD NOT HAVE SUMMONED ME.
I'M AFRAID.
WITH GOOD REASON.

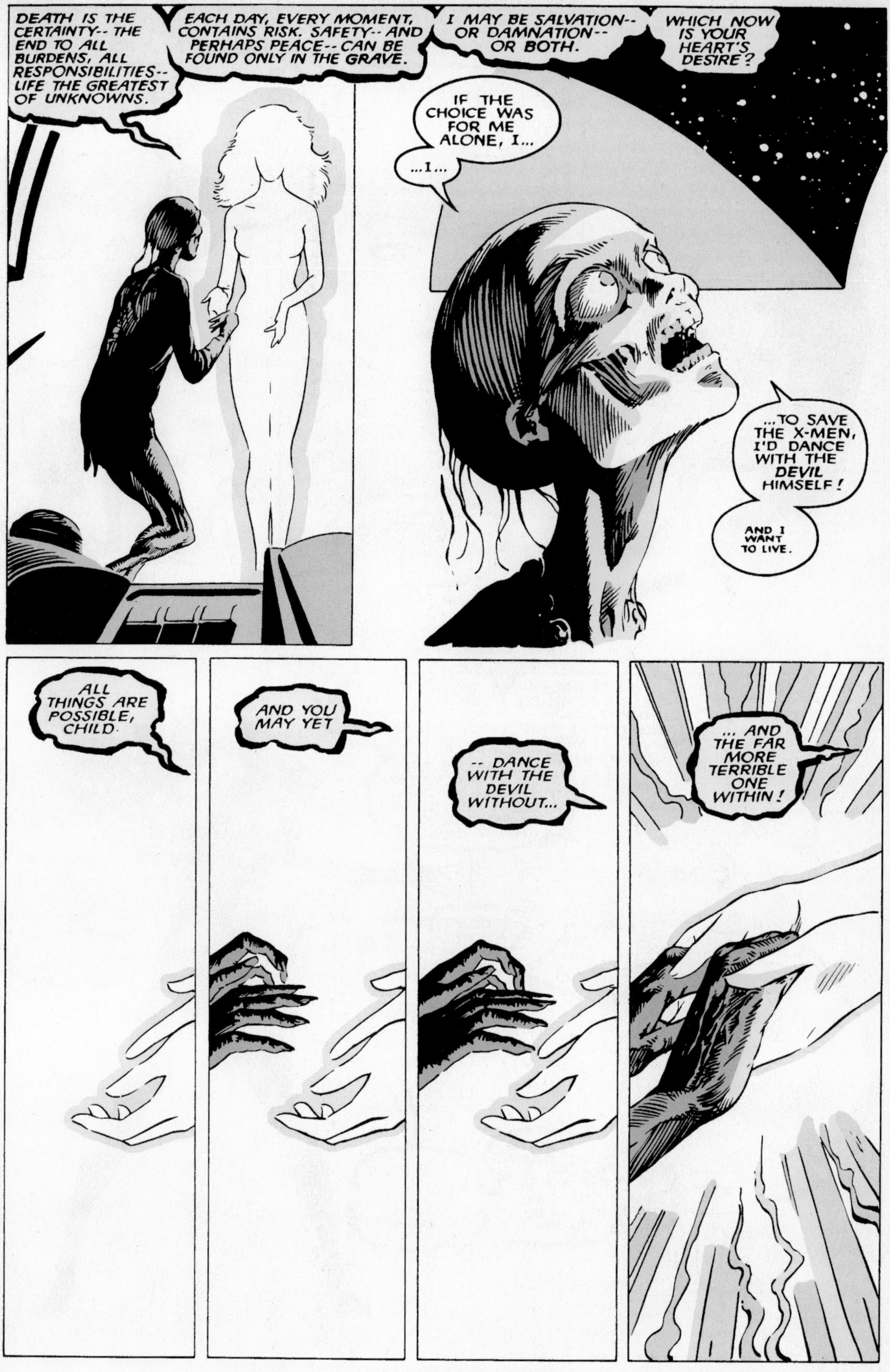
DEATH IS THE CERTAINTY-- THE END TO ALL BURDENS, ALL RESPONSIBILITIES-- LIFE THE GREATEST OF UNKNOWNS.
EACH DAY, EVERY MOMENT, CONTAINS RISK. SAFETY-- AND PERHAPS PEACE-- CAN BE FOUND ONLY IN THE GRAVE.
I MAY BE SALVATION-- OR DAMNATION-- OR BOTH.
WHICH NOW IS YOUR HEART'S DESIRE?
IF THE CHOICE WAS FOR ME ALONE, I...
...I...
...TO SAVE THE X-MEN, I'D DANCE WITH THE DEVIL HIMSELF!
AND I WANT TO LIVE.
ALL THINGS ARE POSSIBLE, CHILD.
AND YOU MAY YET
-- DANCE WITH THE DEVIL WITHOUT...
... AND THE FAR MORE TERRIBLE ONE WITHIN!

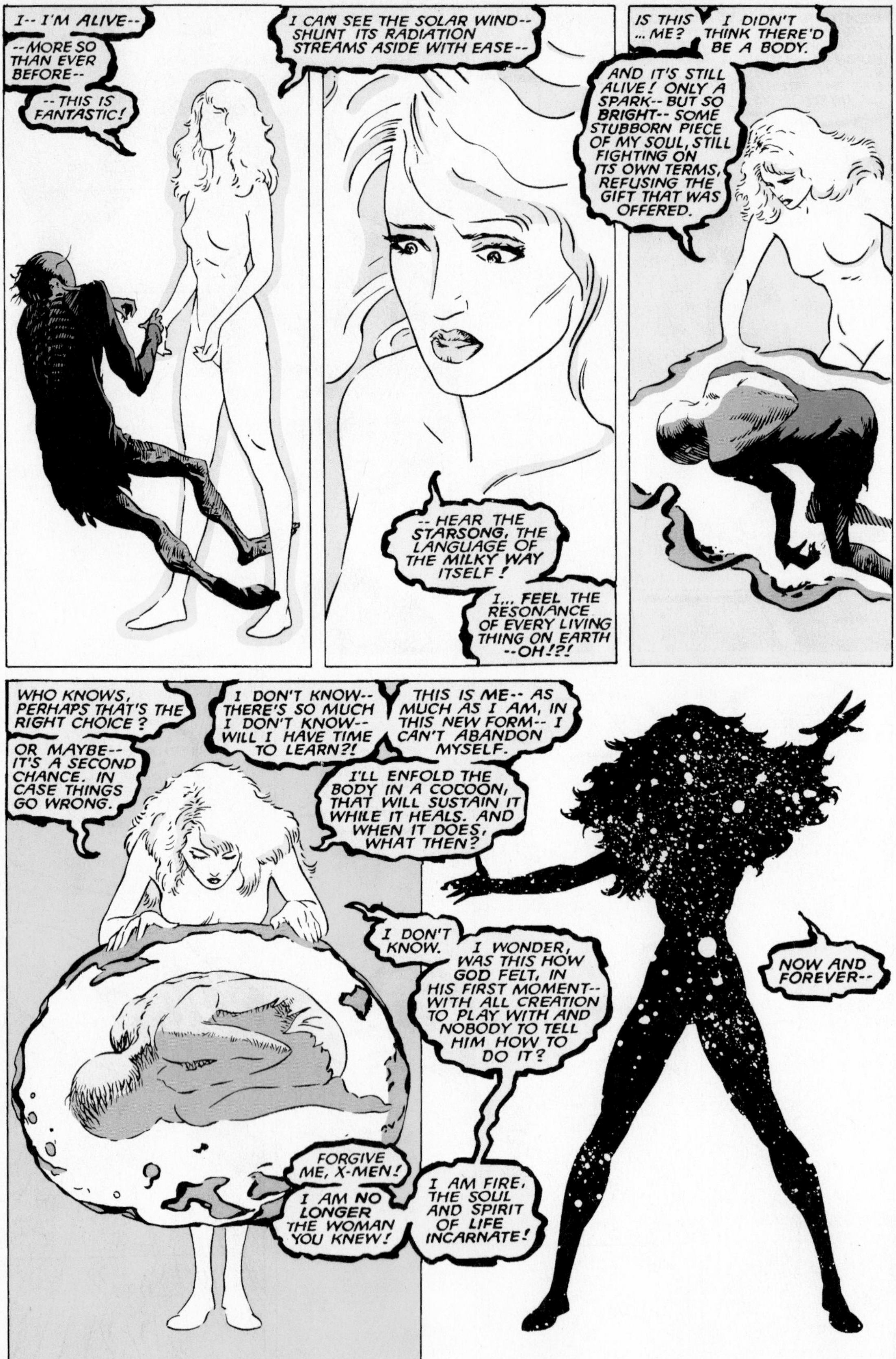
I-- I'M ALIVE--
--MORE SO THAN EVER BEFORE--
--THIS IS FANTASTIC!
I CAN SEE THE SOLAR WIND-- SHUNT ITS RADIATION STREAMS ASIDE WITH EASE--
--HEAR THE STARSONG, THE LANGUAGE OF THE MILKY WAY ITSELF!
I... FEEL THE RESONANCE OF EVERY LIVING THING ON EARTH --OH!?!
IS THIS ... ME?
I DIDN'T THINK THERE'D BE A BODY.
AND IT'S STILL ALIVE! ONLY A SPARK-- BUT SO BRIGHT-- SOME STUBBORN PIECE OF MY SOUL, STILL FIGHTING ON ITS OWN TERMS, REFUSING THE GIFT THAT WAS OFFERED.
WHO KNOWS, PERHAPS THAT'S THE RIGHT CHOICE?
OR MAYBE-- IT'S A SECOND CHANCE. IN CASE THINGS GO WRONG.
I DON'T KNOW-- THERE'S SO MUCH I DON'T KNOW-- WILL I HAVE TIME TO LEARN?!
THIS IS ME-- AS MUCH AS I AM, IN THIS NEW FORM-- I CAN'T ABANDON MYSELF.
I'LL ENFOLD THE BODY IN A COCOON, THAT WILL SUSTAIN IT WHILE IT HEALS. AND WHEN IT DOES, WHAT THEN?
I DON'T KNOW.
I WONDER, WAS THIS HOW GOD FELT, IN HIS FIRST MOMENT-- WITH ALL CREATION TO PLAY WITH AND NOBODY TO TELL HIM HOW TO DO IT?
FORGIVE ME, X-MEN!
I AM NO LONGER THE WOMAN YOU KNEW!
I AM FIRE, THE SOUL AND SPIRIT OF LIFE INCARNATE!
NOW AND FOREVER--

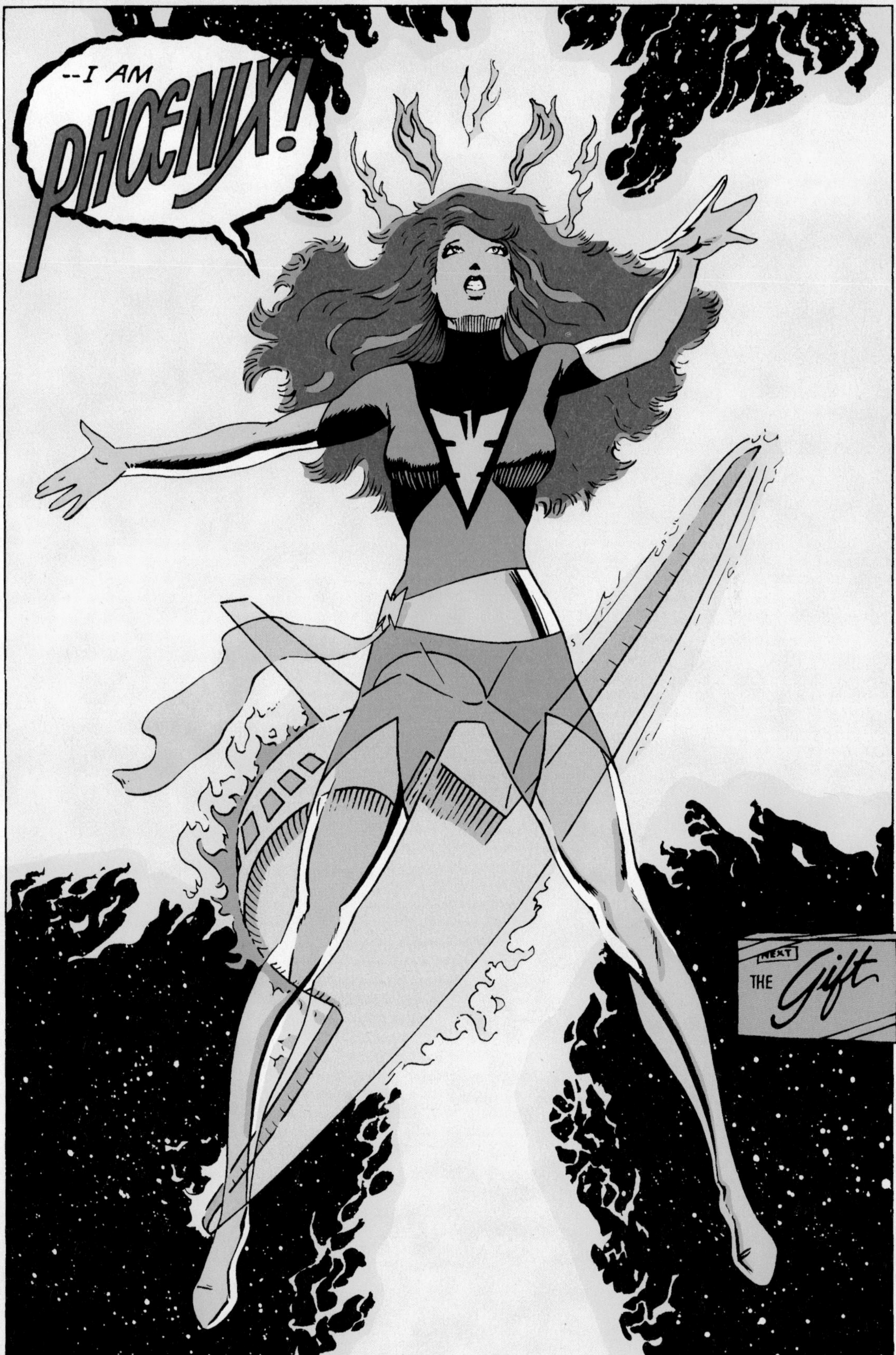
--I AM PHOENIX!
NEXT THE Gift

PORTRAITS AND PATTERNS OF A LIFE.

JEAN GREY'S.

HUMAN. FEMALE. MUTANT. BORN AND RAISED ON EARTH, THE THIRD PLANET OF THE STAR SOL, IN THE GALAXY CALLED THE MILKY WAY.

DIED THERE, TOO, LEAVING NAUGHT BUT THESE FLASHES OF MEMORY:

...THE CHILD JEAN, PSYCHICALLY BONDING TO HER BEST FRIEND AT THE MOMENT OF ANNIE RICHARDSON'S DEATH...

...ENDURING WITH HER THAT FINAL TRAUMA.

A LITTLE OLDER, FIGHTING AS FIERCELY TO SAVE HER MENTOR, PROFESSOR CHARLES XAVIER --

...SCOTT SUMMERS, THE MAN SHE LOVED.

LATER STILL, USING THE POWERS SHE'D WON THAT TERRIBLE DAY TO SAVE ALL CREATION...

...ONLY TO DISCOVER THAT THOSE SELFSAME POWERS WERE BEYOND HER ABILITY TO CONTROL...

-- THEN, ALL GROWN UP, HER FELLOW X-MEN AND MOST ESPECIALLY...

...TRANSFORMING HER FROM THE UNIVERSE'S SAVIOR TO ITS ULTIMATE THREAT.

THAT WAS A ROLE SHE REFUSED TO PLAY.

A LIFE SHE WOULD NOT LIVE.

117

ALL THESE IMAGES... ...RANDOM FRAGMENTS AT THE TIME OF THEIR OCCURRENCE.

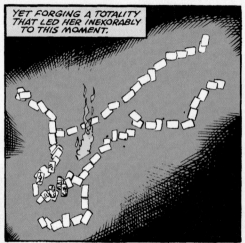

YET FORGING A TOTALITY THAT LED HER INEXORABLY TO THIS MOMENT.

THIS PLACE. EVERYTHING BOUND TOGETHER BY ONE COMMON ELEMENT...

...THE UN-QUENCHABLE, ETERNAL FLAMES OF THE...

AND WHEN THE FIRE FADES...

SCOTT!

HNUNH?

AWAKE?!

ALIVE! BUT HOW!

IT ISN'T *FAIR,* I TRIED SO HARD...

...TO *DIE.*

SPLANG!

♪ ♪ ♪ ♪

UH... ...EXCUSE ME... ...BUT COULD YOU TELL ME PLEASE... ...WHERE I AM?

DUNKA!

MY NAME IS JEAN GREY. I DON'T MEAN TO INTRUDE. BUT I GUESS I'M SORT OF LOST.

CLANKA CLANKA CLANK

SIR-- EXCUSE ME-- --I'D LIKE SOME HELP-- --HEY!

I'M TALKING TO YOU, MISTER!

SO I HEAR, SO WHAT?

ALL I WANT ARE SOME ANSWERS.

WORKIN' CAN'T'CHA SEE! UNIVERSE DON'T REVOLVE ABOUT YOU, SWEETHEART, THERE'S OTHERS TO CONSIDER. ME, I'VE A SCHEDULE TO KEEP, NO TIME FOR IDLE CHIT-CHAT.

IS THERE SOMEONE ELSE I MIGHT--

--OH, THE DEVIL TAKE IT! AND YOU, BUSTER! I'LL FIND THEM MYSELF! SO SORRY TO HAVE BOTHERED YOU, SIR, WON'T I PROMISE HAPPEN AGAIN.

SUIT YOURSELF.

119

"DEVIL TAKE IT" --HAH!

A LINE, ALL THINGS CONSIDERED...

...WITH PAINFUL IMPLICATIONS.

IF THIS IS HADES.

CERTAINLY NOT MY NOTION OF HEAVEN.

HMNH-- MY COSTUME'S CHANGED.

THREE PHASES OF PHOENIX: GREEN WAS THE GOOD ONE...

...RED THE BAD...

...SO WHAT MEANS THIS WHITE?

NICE STARS.

BUT SHOULDN'T THERE BE MORE--

--YAIEEE!

I KNEW THIS WAS A CONSTRUCT--

--I MEAN, THE WORKMAN WAS STARTING ANOTHER FLOOR

(BUT WHY ONLY ONE MAN, ISN'T THERE ANYONE ELSE?)--

--BUT I NEVER IMAGINED IT WOULD LOOK LIKE...

...THIS!

IN THE SKY--

--SWEET MERCY, THOSE AREN'T STARS!

'COURSE THEY ARE, LASS.

IN A MANNER OF SPEAKING.

DON'T PLAY GAMES WITH ME, CURSE YOU--

--THOSE PINPRICKS ARE GALAXIES!

WHAT AM I LOOKING AT OUT THERE, MISTER--

--THE WHOLE UNIVERSE?!

VIEW DOES TAKE SOME GETTING USED TO.

PLEASE-- WHERE AM I?

MY PLACE.

WHAT'S THAT MEAN? YOU BUILD IT, WHY?

WHY NOT? IT'S WHAT I DO.

I'M HALLUCINATING.

GOT TO BE IT. IN SOME BOOBY HATCH SOMEWHERE-- OH, WOULDN'T THAT BE A ROYAL CROCK -- NO MARVEL GIRL, NO X-MEN, NO PHOENIX, JUST THE RAMBLED FANTASIES OF A POOR PSYCHOTIC ALICE WANDERING HAPPILY THROUGH HER OWN LUNATIC SCHIZOPHRENIC WONDERLAND.

OR BETTER YET-- THE MOMENT BEFORE THE END.

WHEN ALL THE CEREBRAL NEURONS FIRE AT ONCE, TO GIVE YOU A WELCOME ILLUSION TO CHECK OUT ON.

WHATEVER WORKS FOR YOU, LASS.

DON'T PATRONIZE ME, BLAST IT!

IF I JUMPED, WHAT WOULD HAPPEN?

YOU'D FALL, Y' SILLY TWIT!

FOREVER!

MY POWERS DIDN'T HOLD ME!

I TRIED TO CATCH MYSELF WITH MY TELE- KINESIS, BUT NOTHING HAPPENED!

MY TELEPATHY'S GONE AS WELL, I CAN'T SENSE ANY THOUGHTS BUT MY OWN!

IT'S BEEN SO LONG...

...SINCE I'VE KNOWN SUCH ...QUIET.

THIS IS SO CRAZY!

WHATEVER. I'VE WORK T' DO.

NO REST FOR THE WEARY, OR THE WICKED.

OR THE *DEAD*?

I DIED ONCE BEFORE, Y'KNOW. I KNOW WHAT IT'S LIKE.

DEATH IS DEATH. WHAT ISN'T, IS LIFE.

ONE OR T'OTHER, NOT BOTH.

WHAT MAKES YOU THE EXPERT?

BEEN AROUND.

TOO MANY TIMES, YOU ASK ME.

LOOK, PAL, I'D LOVE TO STAY AND CHAT BUT

I THINK I NEED

?

BUT I JUST--?!

NEVER MIND, SIMPLY TURN AROUND AND TRY A

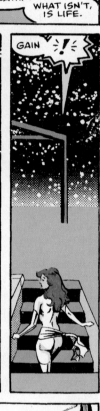

GAIN

WHAT ARE YOU *DOING*?!

MY *JOB*!

AN' THE MORE I TALK WITH YOU, WOMAN, THE LESS I GET DONE. YOU WANT TO MAKE YOURSELF USEFUL, STAY OUT O' MY ROAD AN' STOP BOTHERIN' ME.

ELSEWHERE, PITCH IN AN' LEND A HAND.

BEEN AN AGE SINCE I HAD ME SOME DECENT HELP.

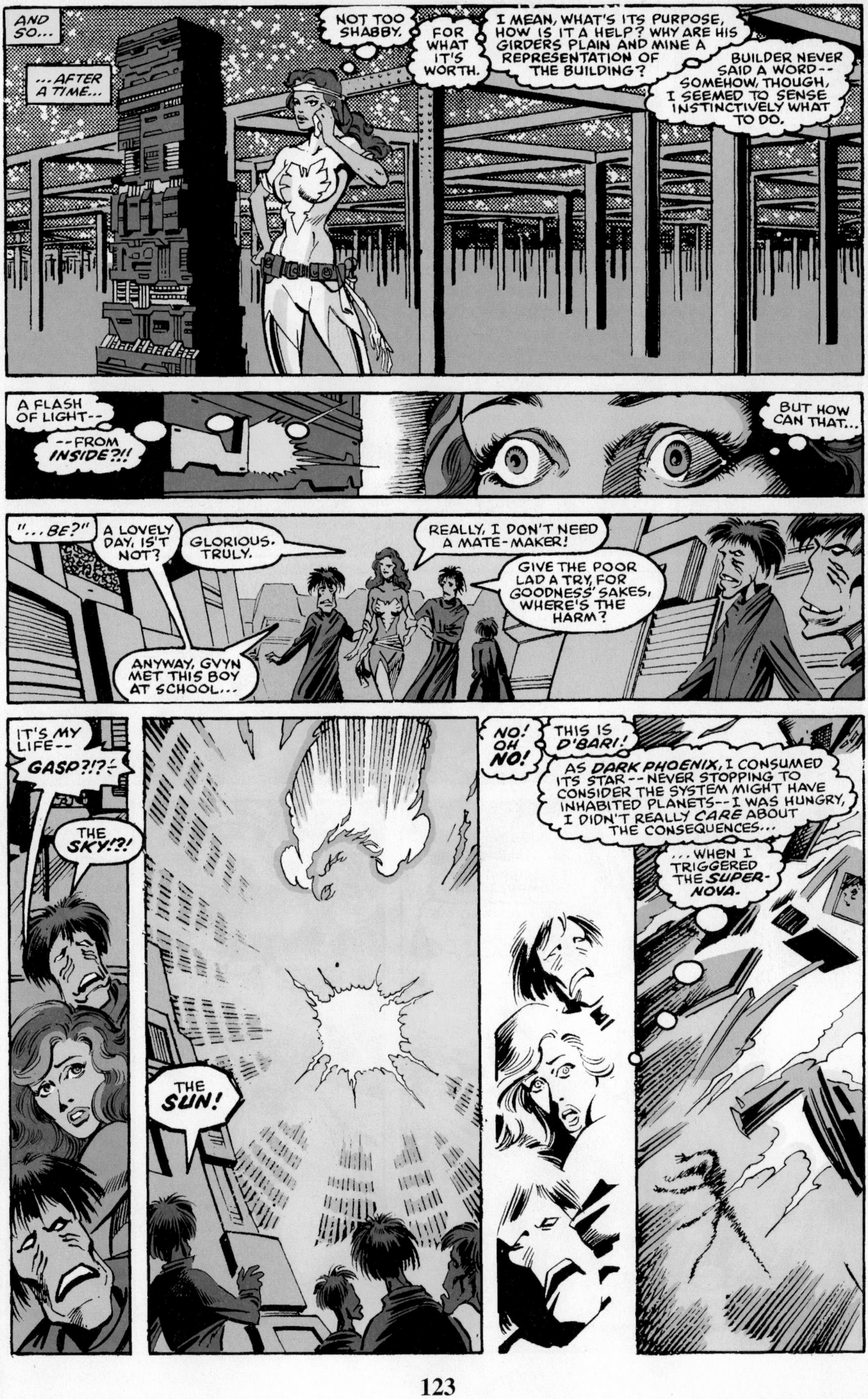
AND SO...
...AFTER A TIME...
NOT TOO SHABBY.
FOR WHAT IT'S WORTH.
I MEAN, WHAT'S ITS PURPOSE, HOW IS IT A HELP? WHY ARE HIS GIRDERS PLAIN AND MINE A REPRESENTATION OF THE BUILDING?
BUILDER NEVER SAID A WORD-- SOMEHOW, THOUGH, I SEEMED TO SENSE INSTINCTIVELY WHAT TO DO.
A FLASH OF LIGHT--
--FROM INSIDE?!!
BUT HOW CAN THAT...
"...BE?"
A LOVELY DAY, IS'T NOT?
GLORIOUS. TRULY.
REALLY, I DON'T NEED A MATE-MAKER!
GIVE THE POOR LAD A TRY, FOR GOODNESS' SAKES, WHERE'S THE HARM?
ANYWAY, GVYN MET THIS BOY AT SCHOOL...
IT'S MY LIFE--
GASP?!?÷
THE SKY!?!
THE SUN!
NO! OH NO!
THIS IS D'BARI!
AS DARK PHOENIX, I CONSUMED ITS STAR--NEVER STOPPING TO CONSIDER THE SYSTEM MIGHT HAVE INHABITED PLANETS--I WAS HUNGRY, I DIDN'T REALLY CARE ABOUT THE CONSEQUENCES...
...WHEN I TRIGGERED THE SUPER-NOVA.

I BURNED! THE WHOLE PLANET-- ALL THOSE POOR PEOPLE--

--WHERE--?!?

THE UNIFORM-- IMPERIAL *SHI'AR!* COULD I BE ABOARD THE STARSHIP...

...I DESTROYED?

YAGKH!

I CALLED THIS *SELF-DEFENSE*, THEY'D FIRED FIRST--

--BUT ONLY BECAUSE, IN THEIR EYES, I'D WANTONLY *EXTERMINATED...*

--AN ENTIRE PLANETARY RACE-- *AAA!*

MY BACK --BONES BREAKING-- TEARING ME UP INSIDE!

TWIN TRACKS OF THOUGHT--

--MY OWN...

...AND THE YOUNG ENSIGN WHOSE LAST MOMENTS...

...I'M RELIVING.

EXPLOSIVE DECOMPRESSION-- --VOIDING ME INTO OPEN SPACE--

--HURTS IT *HURTS* SO SCARED I DON'T WANT TO DIE NO FAIR WHY ME PLEASE MERCY--

--THERE, THE LAST IMAGE SHE SAW-- --IS THAT *ME?!*

DID ALL THIS BRUTALITY--THE WHOLESALE SLAUGHTER-- TRULY GIVES ME...

...SUCH PASSION? SUCH *PLEASURE?!*

NO!

EASY, LASS, EASY.

THE MOMENT'S PASSED.

LET IT GO.

I KNOW YOU.

FINALLY FIGURED THINGS OUT, HAVE YOU?

YOU'RE *DEATH*.

YOU ASKED ME WHERE YOU WERE AND WHAT THIS PLACE IS--

--CONSIDER IT THE *ALPHA* AND *OMEGA*, THE BEGINNING AND END OF *ALL*...

...WHERE THE PHYSICAL UNIVERSE MERGES...

...WITH THE DOMAINS OF THE SPIRIT AND IMAGINATION.

WORDS.

JUST WORDS.

THAT, LASS, MERELY DESCRIBES THE LIMITS OF YOUR PERCEPTION, NOT MY BEING.

GUESS I GOT MY WISH AFTER ALL.

I FINALLY GOT TO *DIE*.

SO TELL ME, MASTER BUILDER, WHICH ROOM ON YOUR EDIFICE IS FOR ME?

IF YOU WERE MEANT FOR HERE, GIRL, YOU'D *BE* HERE.

PART OF ITS FABRIC, AS ARE THOSE IN YOUR SMALL CONTRIBUTION.

NO! IT CAN'T BE, I WON'T HAVE IT-- ARE YOU IMPLYING I'M TO BE YOUR.... APPRENTICE?

AM I *DEATH*, TOO?

I AM THAT I AM.

WHEN I BONDED WITH THE *PHOENIX?*

BUT I *KILLED*-- I MEAN, I JUST *BUILT* A PIECE OF YOUR TOWER--

AND YOU ALREADY MADE YOUR CHOICE.

--WHAT ELSE COULD I BE BUT A PART OF YOU?

WHAT ELSE IS LIFE, BUT A PART OF *DEATH?*

AND DEATH THE *FRAME* THAT GIVES LIFE FORM AND *STRUCTURE?*

THE UNIVERSE REVOLVES ABOUT MY TOWER BECAUSE *OBLIVION* IS WHERE WE BEGIN AND END, NOTHINGNESS TO NOTHINGNESS, WITH THE BRIGHTEST OF FIRES IN BETWEEN.

I BUILD THE *STRUCTURE,* THAT THE PHOENIX MAY CRAFT HER CHAOS, WITHIN AND WITHOUT.

MAKE NO MISTAKE, LASS, YOU'RE *HERS.* BODY AND SOUL.

WHY CAN'T I JUST BE *MINE?* BELONG SOLELY TO *MY-SELF?!*

WHO SAYS THE TWO ARE MUTUALLY EXCLUSIVE?

SINCE CREATION, JEAN, I'VE *NEVER* ENCOUNTERED A CREATURE AS FIERCELY, UNCONQUER-ABLY DEVOTED TO LIFE-- YOU RISKED YOUR OWN TO ENSURE YOUR BEST FRIEND WOULDN'T COME TO ME ALONE.

FAITH, YOU CAST ASIDE YOUR OWN MORTALITY FOR THE SAKE OF THOSE YOU LOVED. SMALL WONDER THE PHOENIX HEARD YOUR CRY, YOU'RE KINDRED SPIRITS.

SO?

D'YOU THINK IT WAS AN *ACCIDENT* THAT, AS A CHILD, YOUR THOUGHTS TOUCHED SCOTT SUMMERS'? OR THAT HE WAS ORPHANED BY THE SHI'AR EMPEROR?

THAT FLEETING CONTACT EVENTUALLY DREW SCOTT TO *PROFESSOR XAVIER'S SCHOOL FOR GIFTED YOUNGSTERS,* WHERE HE GREW INTO *CYCLOPS,* LEADER OF THE *X-MEN.*

HE FELL IN LOVE WITH YOU, AND YOU WITH HIM.

SO THAT, AT THE PROPER TIME AND PLACE, WHEN THAT MAD EMPEROR ATTEMPTED THE OBLITERATION OF *ALL...*

...YOU'D BE THERE TO *STOP* HIM.

IF YOU HANG A *BALANCE,* LASS, TO JUDGE YOURSELF...

...BE SURE TO MEASURE THE COUNTLESS LIVES *SAVED* AS WELL.

YOU SAYING THIS WAS ALL *PRE-ORDAINED?*

WHAT ARE WE, *TOYS* FOR YOUR CELESTIAL AMUSEMENT?

I'M SAYING THAT *SHE* IS THE EMBODIMENT OF LIFE, ITSELF EMBODIED BY *PASSION*--MESSY AND CHAOTIC AND AGONIZING AS THAT CAN BE-- AS I REPRESENT ORDER AND STRUCTURE AND ENTROPY.

AND SHE COULD NOT BEAR TO SEE HER HANDIWORK UNDONE,

SHE REQUIRED A FORM--AN *AVATAR*--THROUGH WHICH TO ACT.

AND WHO BETTER THAN A SPIRIT--A *FIRE,* IF YOU WILL-- CARVED MOST CLOSELY FROM HER OWN.

FINE. BUT WHEN THE JOB WAS DONE, WHY COULDN'T SHE HAVE JUST GONE BACK WHERE SHE CAME FROM AND *LET ME BE?!*

YOU ARE WHERE SHE CAME FROM, DON'T YOU YET UNDERSTAND?

WHEN FIRST YOU MET, YOU CALLED HER A FIGMENT OF YOUR IMAGI- NATION. THAT WASN'T FAR WRONG.

WE ARE *CONCEPTS,* JEAN, DEFINING OURSELVES IN TERMS YOU CAN MOST EASILY COMPREHEND.

THE *PHOENIX* IS NEITHER BEING NOR ENTITY (AS YOU PERCEIVE SUCH THINGS)...

...IT IS A *FORCE.*

THE SUM AND SUBSTANCE OF *ALL THAT LIVES.*

YOUR *UNIQUE* GIFT IS TO BE THE ONE CAPABLE OF WIELDING THAT FORCE. IT CAME TO YOU, JEAN--AS IT WILL IN TIME TO YOUR CHILDREN--BECAUSE, LIKE THE SWORD *EXCALIBUR* WAS TO KING ARTHUR...

IT IS YOURS BY *RIGHT.*

WHETHER I WANT IT OR NOT?

IF YOU HADN'T WANTED IT, YOU WOULDN'T HAVE CALLED. IF IT HADN'T BEEN *MEANT* FOR YOU... IT WOULDN'T HAVE ANSWERED.

TOO BAD.

I'D HOPED--SELFISHLY--THERE WERE *TWO* OF US, THAT I'D BEEN *POSSESSED* BY SOME FRIGHTFUL CREATURE I COULD BLAME FOR WHAT HAPPENED.

PASSION IS A TWO- EDGED BLADE. WITH THE FINEST OF LINES BETWEEN THE LIGHT AND THE SHADOW.

BUT WHEN THE SCALES LIFTED...

...THE BALANCE CAME DOWN ON THE SIDE OF *LOVE.*

COLD COMFORT, I'M AFRAID.

A HARD LESSON, AYE, BUT YOU'RE LEARNING.

WHO PAYS THE PRICE WHILE I'M IN SCHOOL?

I SWORE, NO MORE BLOOD ON MY HANDS. I MEAN THAT!

YOUR LIFE, YOUR POWER, YOUR RESPONSIBILITY.

TO WHERE? SALVATION, DAMNATION-- WHICH?

WHAT'S NEXT FOR ME, WHERE DO I GO FROM HERE?!

YOUR CHOICES, ALL THE WAY.

WHEREVER-- WHATEVER-- COMES NATURALLY.

I CAN HEAR AGAIN! IN MY MIND!

THE LIFE-FORCE-- THE COSMOS--SINGS THROUGH ME LIKE MUSIC!

THE BEAUTY--THE GLORY--IT'S INDESCRIBABLE!

I'M SCARED.

IT'S A HARD PATH BEFORE YOU. NO QUESTION.

RISKS AS GREAT--TEMPTA-TIONS ABOUNDING--AS THE REWARDS ARE AWFUL.

ONE FEEDS DESIRE, THE OTHER LAYERS ON RESPONSIBILITY.

NO WAY TO KNOW THE DIFFERENCE TILL YOU'RE AT THE CROSSROADS.

AND IF I SCREW UP?

LEARN, GROW. DO BETTER.

I WON'T FORGET YOU, FRIEND.

OR OUR TALK.

THIS TIME, TRUST ME, THINGS'LL TURN OUT RIGHT.

TAKE CARE!

YOU, TOO. POOR WEE THING.

IF ONLY IT WERE THAT EASY.

EVERY CREATURE BORN--EVEN A BABY *PHOENIX*--

--REACHES A MOMENT WHERE IT HAS TO STRIKE OUT ON ITS OWN.

THE SADNESS BEING THAT THE MOSAIC OF LIFE CONTAINS MORE PIECES THAN YOU KNOW.

THINGS YOU CAN'T BE TOLD, BUT HAVE TO DISCOVER FOR YOURSELF, NO MATTER THE COST.

I'M TRULY SORRY, CHILD, YOU'LL REMEMBER NEITHER WORDS, NOR ME.

BUT YOU WILL LEARN.

THE *HARD* WAY.

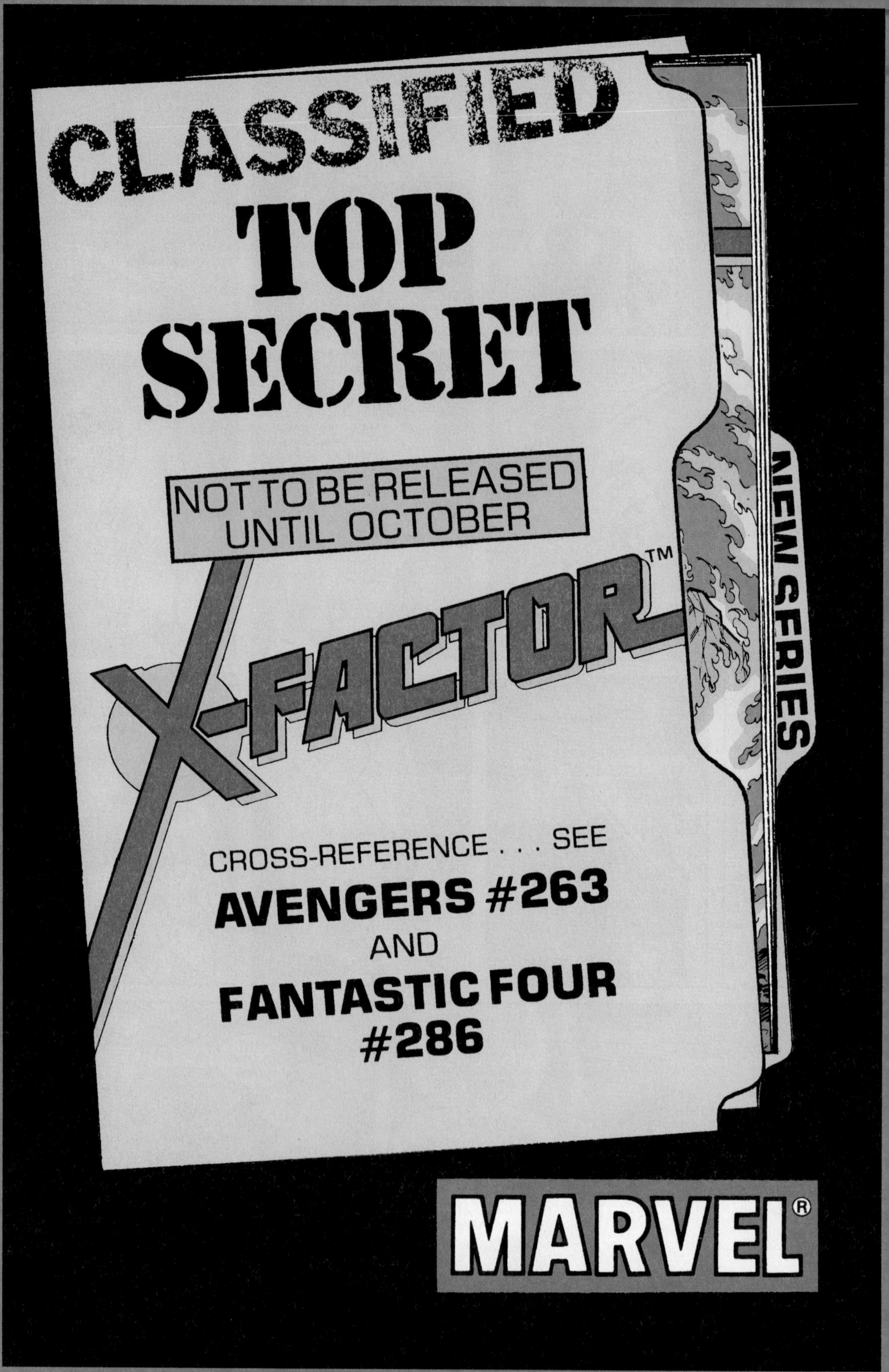
CLASSIFIED
TOP SECRET
NOT TO BE RELEASED UNTIL OCTOBER
X-FACTOR™
NEW SERIES
CROSS-REFERENCE . . . SEE
AVENGERS #263
AND
FANTASTIC FOUR #286
MARVEL®

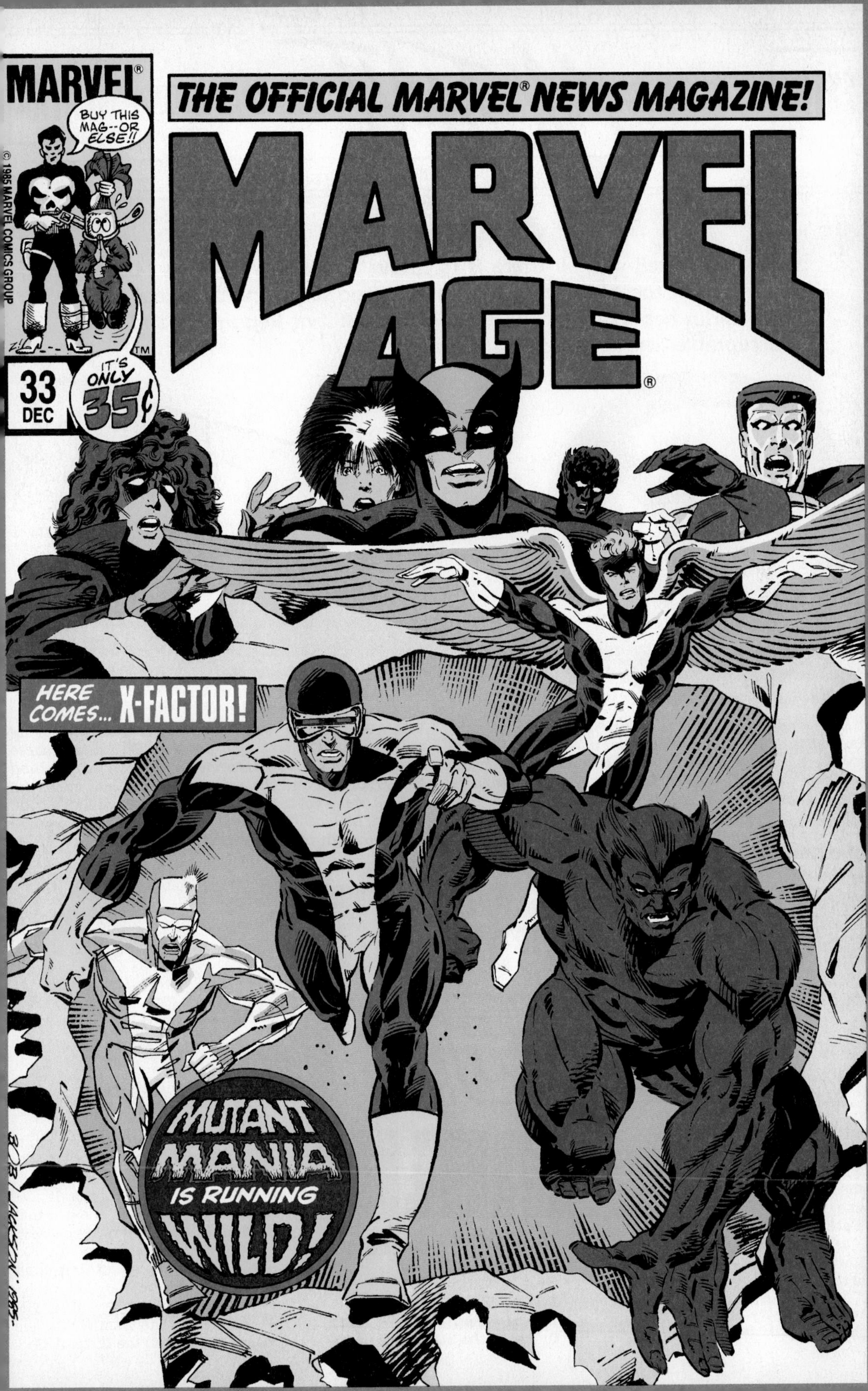

MARVEL®
BUY THIS MAG--OR ELSE!!
© 1985 MARVEL COMICS GROUP
TM
33 DEC
IT'S ONLY 35¢
THE OFFICIAL MARVEL® NEWS MAGAZINE!
MARVEL AGE®
HERE COMES... X-FACTOR!
MUTANT MANIA IS RUNNING WILD!

THE *MUTANT* REPORT

VOLUME 1   "The Next Step in News Evolution!"   NUMBER 4

CLASSIFIED!

We'd like to tell you all there is to know about X-FACTOR . . . but we can't! It's just too big, too momentous . . . too surprising to reveal all! So Mike Carlin has *screened* this issue of *The Mutant Report* . . . and made it acceptable for human eyes!

Everyone in the office is talking about it. Everyone in fandom, it seems, is asking about it. And occasionally, just occasionally, it seems like everyone in comics is working on it! What is it? Why, merely the return of the original X-Men in their own series as the all-new, all-amazing X-Factor, that's what!

We've been dropping hints about X-FACTOR here and there, but now that it's time to do the X-FACTOR MAR-VEL AGE preview, we're determined to do something really special! So we've got not one, not two, not three or even four—but six interviews with the gang behind X-FACTOR #1 and the amazing events that surround it! Plus, we've got behind-the-scenes looks at how a book is born, including design sketches and unused covers!

But enough of this verbiage! You want info ... here you go!

MIKE FACTOR ONE CARLIN

Aside from being the editor of such comics as FANTASTIC FOUR and DAZZLER, Mike happens to be the editor of, and one of the movers and shakers behind, X-FACTOR. Here's what he has to say . . .

Mike, I'd like to get from you the low-down on this, the most-talked about series since SECRET WARS. I know nothing—nothing!

Surely you know who X-Factor is?

Bob Layton and Jackson Guice are X-Factor.

What is X-Factor?

X-FACTOR is a comic book.

Why is X-FACTOR?

To get to the other side. X-FAC-TOR is a comic book series reuniting—let me rephrase that—X-FACTOR is a new concept in team super heroic comic books. It features the X-Men—yes, the original X-Men. All the rumors are correct.

Jean Grey comes back?

What?! No Comment. But don't quote me.

Who are the members exactly?

Members of the team will be the Beast, the Angel, the Iceman, Cyclops and [redacted]

It sounds interesting! How did the concept of X-FACTOR come about?

The concept is actually Bob Layton's idea, with a lot of help from Jackson Guice and Jim Shooter. Bob had been looking for a regular feature to do since his HERCULES Limited Series ended. He's a big fan of the original X-Men, as I am. The current mutant-mania in the Marvel Universe is the prime factor in getting X-Factor together.

Some of the members will be coming from the new Defenders. How will that affect that team?

The New Defenders will have broken up by the time X-Factor is formed. Thus the three ex-Defenders will have nothing to do until X-Factor comes along.

Why is X-Factor formed?

Their *raison d'etre* is that they are going to try and help the mutants of the world.

A lot of the mutants living on Earth, you see, are just regular men and women with regular jobs. They are not super heroes or super villains. They are just different. To help these mutants, X-Factor is going to form a mutant hunting firm. X-Factor is going to become an advertised commodity for people who are afraid of mutants. They can call this special confidential number and turn in their neighbor or anyone else they believe is a mutant. X-Factor will then come in and "capture" these "dangerous" mutants and either "eliminate" them or de-mutantize them.

What do you mean by de-mutantize them?

Basically it is a sound-and-light show to fool the humans. In reality, X-Factor is going to train the mutants on how to control their abilities and keep what they are secret from the rest of the world. So the de-mutantizing is actually a way of teaching the mutants how to cope in a world becoming more hysterical about the mutant menace.

It seems strange that X-Factor, a band of mutants, would be hunting other mutants.

X-Factor figures that the best way to remain hidden is to be in the middle of the mutant spotlight, so to speak, posing as a mutant hunting organization for hire—a bounty-hunting organization with a twist.

When will the forming of X-Factor happen?

The first sign of anything happening will be in THE AVENGERS #263. That is where the Avengers will run across a kind of energy cocoon at the bottom of Jamaica Bay. They will dredge this cocoon up and not know what is inside it. At first they will think [redacted] But it will not [redacted]

The very next week after that, in FANTASTIC FOUR #286, Reed Richards will open the cocoon and find out who and what is inside. [redacted] is inside.

Now Reed's problem is this: Is this [redacted] or is this [redacted] The Fantastic Four will eventually contact the New Defenders because that is where the Angel and all her friends are.

The story then picks up in X-FACTOR #1. So the beginning of X-FACTOR is a three-way cross-over.

You already answered why X-Factor is formed, but not how.

Basically, the discovery of [redacted] will be the catalyst for X-Factor forming. [redacted] And that meeting will leave Scott Summers emotionally devastated. [redacted]

Why so?

Well, right now the world is almost totally against mutants—hates them with a passion. [redacted]

*Preliminary character designs for **X-FACTOR**—for the final versions, see our cover.*

██████ let the situation get this bad. ██████ do something to right the wrong being committed against mutantkind—

That's a task difficult for a team —virtually impossible for one person.

██████ Scott, unfortunately for him, will be so distraught ██████ —that he will be incapable of any rational action for some time. The Angel, however, after he gets over his surprise, will offer to help ██ Because he is independently wealthy, and has many contacts, he will be the backer for X-Factor. He'll contact the Beast and Iceman and they will quickly join the team.

What's going to be their first mission?

In the first issue, they will come across a young mutant who severely needs their help. He doesn't know how to control his powers. And unless X-Factor can help him, he will be unable to stop an incredible horror from being unleashed within him.

Will there be much tie-in with what is happening in THE X-MEN and THE NEW MUTANTS?

Of course there will be X-Men continuity involved, but basically we are going to be starting fresh. It's a whole new direction for these characters. By posing as a business, they will have become so underground that they are overground. As I said earlier, they've hidden themselves by placing themselves directly in the public eye.

How about enemies? Surely they will begin to have some other than mankind at large?

There will be villains—most of them new. As we do more stories, we are going to discover who is their arch-enemy.

Are their adventures going to be primarily in one area, or will they be traveling the world?

X-Factor is going to globe-trot a little bit. They are really going to take the fate of all mutant-dom into their hands. Sometimes mutants they encounter won't want to be helped—and sometimes the mutants they are hunting will be villains. There will be a wide variety of stories, that we can guarantee.

Considering that the members of X-Factor have been together before in the X-Men, I'd like to go down the roster and get comments from you about how they will be presented in X-FACTOR.

Okay, but I can't guarantee how much I'm going to say.

An unused cover. Who's in the middle? Take a guess!

I understand. The first name is Scott Summers—Cyclops. Is he, and the other members for that matter, going to keep his original designation?

Yes. But they won't be using them very much. They will be using their regular real names, not their old X-Men names.

With Scott, he will now be ██ the ██████ ██████ caused ██████ ██████ This is his dilemma.

Because he will be going through so many personal problems, he will not be the leader of X-Factor. Scott will ██████

██████ but that will only make things more complicated for him.

Speaking of ██████ what of ██████?

██ is the one ██████ ██████ Unlike the others, ██████ ██████ is gone.

What about ██████ that you mentioned earlier?

██████ ██████ ██████ will soon become obvious.

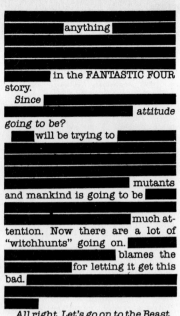

███ anything ███

███ in the FANTASTIC FOUR story. *Since* ███ *attitude going to be?*

███ will be trying to ███.

███ mutants and mankind is going to be ███

███ much attention. Now there are a lot of "witchhunts" going on. ███ blames the ███ for letting it get this bad. ███

All right. Let's go on to the Beast.

The Beast will go through some changes himself. He is going to begin to de-fur and eventually get back to the way he used to look. He will be doing the scientific research for the team, since his background was in science. He will also start to use big words again.

How about Iceman?

Iceman will probably not make any more ice bridges.

Why not?

Only because of the potential lawsuits involved with ice bridges that would later melt and collapse on people or property. He is also going to ███ Iceman is basically the same happy-go-lucky fellow he's always been. He will be along for the ride, in many respects. But not too long after he joins X-Factor, something weird will happen to him in a foreign country that will cause a big change in his life.

Let's move on to the Angel.

Fine. He's the financial backer for the group. And he is the producer—the one who gets things done.

Is he going to ███

Possibly.

You mentioned that X-Factor will be using "a sound-and-light show" to de-mutantize mutants. What do you mean exactly?

Well, X-Factor, because they are going to be a bona-fide organization, are going to have everything that anyone would expect a mutant-hunting outfit to have.

They'll have sophisticated transportation, a high-tech office building and mutant de-activating equipment. The thing is, the de-activating equipment is just something that will produce a good show for the onlookers. It will appear as if something is being done to nullify the mutant abilities. But the stuff is all placebo.

How long will this sort of wool-pulling last?

As long as Professor X's academy has lasted without humans knowing its true nature. X-Factor is much more public, but they have the money to cover their trail.

What about cross-overs and guest-stars from other members of the Marvel Universe?

We will have guest-stars. Nothing is planned quite yet, except for Reed Richards and the Avengers in the first issue.

What are your feelings about X-FACTOR?

It is the biggest collaboration since SECRET WARS. It is also a lot harder because it is going to turn into a series, and not just have a limited run. I am really happy that X-FACTOR is happening. I like all the characters, was a big fan of them when they were the original X-Men. I feel honored to be a part of their resurgence for a whole new generation.

BOB FACTOR TWO LAYTON

From IRON MAN to HERCULES, the name of Bob Layton has always been associated with the best Marvel has to offer. Now Bob takes on his first monthly series as both writer and inker!

Bob, how did you and Jackson Guice create X-FACTOR?

I did it the way I do everything. Jim Shooter told me to do it.

Were you a fan of the original X-Men?

Yeah.

You are going to be both writing and inking the series, correct?

Actually, Jackson and I will be co-plotting the stories and in a few cases, switching roles on each other. So at any given time, I might be penciling and Jackson inking, and vice-versa.

How long did it take you to create a rational explanation for the ███

███

There is no ███ She's dead.

Mike told me that Scott Summers is going to be really in a blue funk over ███

Mike talks too much. And you ask too many questions.

Jim Salicrup told me to do that. The X-Factor is going to be composed ███ *members of the original X-Men. Are you going to add any new members?*

That's for me to know and you to find out—in the comic.

What are your feelings about working with Jackson Guice?

Jackson is probably one of the hottest new talents—bar none—in the business. With all of what he's done—you haven't seen anything yet. When people see what he's doing in X-FACTOR, they will know what I mean when I say that I think he is the best new talent to appear in the industry in years. He and I are a great mesh. Our styles are similar and when the comic hits the stands, people's eyes are going to pop out.

What is the overall tone that you want to set with X-FACTOR?

The truth of the matter is, I don't want to spoil X-FACTOR for the reader by telling him too much about what will be happening before he actually sees it. Every issue will be a surprise and a shock.

Will they be traveling to different parts of the Earth?

No comment.

Any final words?

If you like the original X-Men, you will love X-FACTOR.

JACKSON FACTOR THREE* GUICE

X-Factor is a first for Jackson as, well! Although he's garnered piles of praise for his powerful penciling on such books as THE MICRO-NAUTS and SWORDS OF THE SWASHBUCKLERS, this will be his first straight-forward super hero adventure title, and boy, is he enthusiastic!

Bob credits you both with creating X-FACTOR. Can you tell us its genesis?

Bob and I were simply sitting around at Marvel, discussing various books. We were also reminiscing about some of the comics we enjoyed when we were growing up. The subject got around to the original X-Men. We casually mentioned to editor-in-chief Jim Shooter that he should put the original X-Men back together in their own book. One thing led to another and that's what happened.

Had you and Bob ever worked together before?

X-FACTOR is the first thing that we're doing steadily together. We had been talking off and on about doing a project together for some time, but nothing had ever come of it. Then when we mentioned to Jim Shooter the idea of reviving the original X-Men as a team and Jim said, "Well, when can the both of you start?" That's when we looked at each other and decided that maybe now was the time to finally do something together—and that X-FACTOR was the something we should do.

What sort of feel do you want to establish with X-FACTOR?

Well, this is the first real super hero book that I've done since I started working at Marvel. This is my first opportunity to do a real mainline super hero comic for Marvel. I was raised on the early Marvel super heroes and I'd like to bring that sort of Jack Kirby feel and excitement to X-FACTOR.

How will your work for X-FAC-TOR compare with what you are doing on THE SWORDS OF THE SWASHBUCKLERS?

Well, with SWASHBUCKLERS, writer Bill Mantlo and I are really trying to go back and capture the feel of pirate adventure and the old style of illustration. The inking style I am using on SWASHBUCK-LERS is kind of heavy by today's standards. But it gives the series more of a wood-cut or old-style illustrative look. In X-FACTOR, I am going to try and do the good, clean, solid, punchy super hero comic book story-telling.

Bob mentioned the fact that you and he plan to switch artistic roles occasionally.

That's right. I like to keep my hand in inking. And Bob is so excited about X-FACTOR that he

Another preliminary design, sans fifth member.

---

*And how many original X-MEN fans get that reference?

wants to pencil some of the issues. So we plan to, every so often, switch off and reverse artistic jobs.

There is a huge cloak of secrecy surrounding one of X-FACTOR's members, ██████████. How did ████████ come about?

It was John Byrne, Roger Stern, and Kurt Busiek who had the original idea to ████████████████████ And as X-FACTOR was being planned that idea was put forth. Originally Bob and I thought about doing that in the 10th or 12th issue. But the decision soon evolved into opening the series with that bombshell. There was a big editorial meeting. Mike Carlin, Jim Shooter, Bob Layton, John Byrne and Roger Stern were all locked up in Jim's office and it was then that they hashed out what would happen in X-FACTOR #1 and the cross-overs with THE AVENGERS and the FANTASTIC FOUR.

What sort of adventures will X-Factor be having?

There will be an international feel to X-FACTOR. They are going to be traveling all over the world in their search for mutants. They will be in Europe, possibly the South Pacific. Plans are pretty vague right now. We just have a lot of different countries we want them to go to.

We're trying to convince Marvel to send us to all these countries so we can get on-the-spot reference — especially to places like Tahiti. (Laughter.)

The Bullpen has really been blown away with your pencils on X-FACTOR. How do you rate your own work on the series?

I feel that my X-FACTOR art is the best stuff I've done yet. It's the material I'm most pleased with so far. Working with Bob and Mike Carlin on the series has been really great—they've given me my best working relationship in comics. Everything has really clicked together for us, and I guess that is showing in the work. I hope that X-FACTOR goes over real well and that everyone likes what we're doing.

ROGER FACTOR FOUR STERN

As the AVENGERS scribe, Roger is in the enviable position of kicking off the three-way cross-over that begins the X-FACTOR series! Here's how Earth's mightiest heroes got into the act . . .

Roger, how and when did you create the concept that has proved so pivotal in X-FACTOR?

Actually, it spun off of an idea that MARVEL AGE MAGAZINE Assistant Editor Kurt Busiek mentioned to me about two or three years ago. We were sitting around talking and he said, "You know, I've thought of a way to ████████ ████" I told him, "No, no, we'd never want to ████████████████" He said "Not ████████████ What if ████████ What if ████████████████ ?" I told him, "That's a dandy idea!" I later mentioned this to John Byrne later and we kicked it around a few times. Then when we heard that Bob Layton was doing X-FACTOR, John told the idea to Bob and everything started to move.

What happened then?

I was called to a big meeting. Jim Shooter, Bob Layton, John Byrne, Mike Carlin, Mark Gruenwald and myself were all in Jim's office to discuss the plot for X-FACTOR #1 and cross-over stories for THE AVENGERS and THE FANASTIC FOUR. It evolved that I would get the ball rolling in THE AVENGERS, John would pick it up in THE FAN-TASTIC FOUR and then it would all get tied-up in X-FACTOR.

What will happen in THE AVENGERS?

It's the set-up of the mystery of what is at the bottom of ████████ ████ Other things will be happening in the story, but basically the Avengers will discover there is something at the bottom of ████████

It's Genetic
"HUMOR IN A MUTATED VEIN"   by **Kyle Baker**

that is causing a big disturbance. They will fish out this object and return with it to Avengers Mansion. The big revelation of what's inside will happen in THE FANASTIC FOUR.

This must be calling for some pretty close coordinating with John Byrne and Bob Layton.

It is. John and I have been burning up the phone lines. And I've talked to Bob a number of times. Mike Carlin, the editor of both X-FACTOR and THE FANTASTIC FOUR has been doing the major share of making sure things stayed on track. As for John and myself, we've been doing a lot of cross-over action between the Avengers and the Fantastic Four, anyway, because they all happen to be living in the same building right now.

That's right, the FF don't have a home because the Baxter Building was destroyed.

Right. John called me up earlier today because he wanted to make sure the Avengers had working Quinjets because there is this thing coming up in THE AVENGERS where the Federal Aviation Administration has told the Avengers that they can't have the Quinjets at the mansion anymore. I told him that in my story, the FAA had given them 30 days notice. John said, "Great, then they can use the Quinjet for this thing they have to do."

How do you feel about being the lead-off writer in this trilogy of cross-overs?

I'm pleased as punch. I always loved the original X-Men. To be one of the prime movers in refounding the original concept in a new book is just great. Cross-overs can be difficult sometimes, coordinating all the different elements and making sure they come out in the right order is demanding. But this one has been real fun. I can't wait to see it come out.

JOHN FACTOR FIVE BYRNE

The writer/penciler of the first series in the Marvel Age of Comics is in on welcoming the newest, too! What does the Fantastic Four have to do with X-Factor? Read on!

John, how did the Fantastic Four get wrapped up in the mystery?

They got involved for two reasons: 1) because I wanted to be involved with X-FACTOR and I am doing the Fantastic Four and 2) because the Avengers bring the object they discover ▇▇▇▇▇▇ back to Avengers Mansion where the FF are also staying. When you have Reed Richards around, no mysterious object stays uninvestigated for long. He very quickly discovers that there's more to this object than meets the eye. Reed manages to determine that there is a ▇▇▇▇▇▇ in the object in ▇▇▇▇▇▇ apparently very close to

A human being or a life force?

A human being. He knows that the thing inside is human. He found that out with the help of Sue, his wife. He had her use her power to make visible things invisible on the featureless cocoon. Sue is able to penetrate the cocoon, not very well, but enough so that they get a quick glimpse inside. They manage to see ▇▇▇▇▇▇ Their next step is to determine ▇▇▇▇▇▇

What happens then?

Reed sets up a bio-radiant stimulator to try and coax the being inside the cocoon to full consciousness. This works a lot better than he had hoped.

How have coordinating your efforts with Roger and Bob gone?

Basically, it has been pretty easy. Bob, Roger and myself had this big meeting with Jim Shooter, Mike Carlin and Mark Gruenwald. That's where we hammered out what would happen. It was a lot of fun for me because I haven't seriously plotted with somebody else in about five years. My role in plotting anything has been kind of to be the devil's advocate in order to stimulate the other person to come up with the best idea he possibly can.

it's not as much fun when I do that to myself.

Speaking of you plotting with another person, Roger mentioned that it was you who actually brought the pivotal concept, the one that roped in the Avengers and the FF, to Bob Layton. Could you tell us what happened?

The first thing I did when Roger told me the idea was to talk to Chris Claremont about the idea. ███████ ████████████ Then, when I heard about X-Factor, I went straight to Bob Layton and said, "███████ ██████████████ Here is the way ███████████

What was Bob's reaction when you told him?

He went nuts. He loved it. We immediately set about scrapping entirely Bob's first issue and reworking it to include this idea and also figuring out how Roger and I, who were the main movers and shakers for it, to get a piece of it for ourselves. Eventually, the two set-ups, starting with THE AVENGERS, evolved.

How has the story been going for you?

I'm having a lot of fun with the Fantastic Four part of it. This particular issue is going to be 30 pages with no ads—a special issue. And the storyline is one of those weird situations where for some reason it all just feels right. Everything seems to fit and doesn't contradict anything previously established.

Have you seen any of Jackson Guice's art for X-FACTOR #1?

Yes, and it looks great. I'm going to have to break Jackson's hands one of these days. (Laughter.) His figures tend to be long and attenuated which sort of makes him the "El Greco" of Marvel. He is calling what he does on X-FACTOR "breakdowns" but I would call it full pencils, myself. It just—everything you want to see is right there on the page. I should think that the finished product is going to be really sweet. For anybody who is ready for the next X-Men book, this one is it. And it is ███████ with

JIM
FACTOR SIX
SHOOTER

For the final word on X-FACTOR, who better than our Editor in Chief, the guy who oversees everything here at the House of Ideas? Jim has not only been closely involved in the creation of X-FACTOR, but no one is more qualified than he to judge X-FACTOR's impact, both on Marvel Comics and the Marvel Universe.

As Bob and Jackson recalled, you were instrumental in getting X-FACTOR off the ground, Jim.

I'm sure I contributed little bits and pieces to X-FACTOR, but basically most of the credit should go to Bob Layton if for no other reason than it was his dogged persistence that led to X-FACTOR becoming a reality.

The big conference that defined what would happen in the three-way cross-over went over incredibly well, judging from everyone's comments. Could you describe your role in it?

We went through the plots for THE AVENGERS, THE FANTASTIC FOUR and the first couple issues of X-FACTOR and I did what I always do in these situations; I was the enforcer of craft. I was the one who made very certain that things were explained properly to the readers, that there was a real good conflict evolving in that first issue and that there would be a big climax. As for the rest, I mostly let the others come up with the real creative stuff. The result is something which I think is very good.

When you mentioned explanations, they appear especially critical considering what is planned to happen.

Yes, definitely. This is a book that I think is going to be a real milestone in Marvel history. I think it will be remembered as a significant event in the same way that the issue of DAREDEVIL that had the death of Elektra was a significant event, in the same way the death of Phoenix was a significant event. X-FACTOR #1 ranks with the first coming of Galactus, it ranks with the SECRET WARS sagas. Therefore I was very, very insistent we do it well.

What do you feel will be X-FACTOR's contribution to the Mutant Mythos?

I think that X-FACTOR is a natural evolutionary development within our ongoing Marvel Mythos—especially the mutant part of the Marvel Mythos. Now all three generations of X-Men are accounted for. There are the New Mutants who are the current class in school, there are the uncanny X-Men who are the current grad students/student-teachers and strike force. But for years there were the questions: What happened to the old grads? What about the first graduating class? Where are those guys? Well, now there is a book that deals with them. All three generations of mutants that we have seen are now coming forth in their own right. And I think that what has happened is something very natural, it will fit right in. And considering the events going on in THE X-MEN right now, X-FACTOR was necessary.

Could you elaborate?

If you have been reading THE X-MEN, you know that there have been some incredible happenings taking place. The unthinkable has happened! Magneto is now with the X-Men, furthermore, at the helm! And if you consider that it is a shock to readers who have seen Magneto, up close and personal, try to kill the X-Men so many times—not to mention the Avengers, the Fantastic Four, Thor and quite a few others—just imagine how much of a shock it is to Cyclops, for Iceman, the Beast and the Angel—for people who were there fighting him from the very beginning.

So what's going on in X-FACTOR is a very direct, very natural outgrowth of the events taking place in THE X-MEN. We think all the ramifications through, then we tell the story the way it should be. That's what the Marvel Universe is all about.

— *Dwight Jon Zimmerman*

IN 1986, MARVEL EDITOR IN CHIEF JIM SHOOTER REQUESTED LAST-MINUTE CHANGES
TO THE *PHOENIX RISING* STORYLINE THAT WERE SCRIPTED BY CHRIS CLAREMONT
AND DRAWN BY JACKSON GUICE. SEVERAL OF THE PAGES AS ORIGINALLY WRITTEN AND
ILLUSTRATED BY JOHN BYRNE FOR *FANTASTIC FOUR #286* HAVE SURFACED THROUGH
THE YEARS AND ARE PRESENTED HERE. SCANS COURTESY OF BRIAN PECK.

I... I CAN'T *MOVE.* WHAT HAVE YOU DONE TO ME?

PLEASE! PLEASE! MY *FRIENDS!* THEY'RE DEPENDING ON ME.

THEY'LL *DIE!!*

I CHOSE *WELL,* JEAN GREY. YOUR OWN FIRES ARE *STRONG.* YOU MAKE A WORTHY *IMAGE* FOR ME.

BUT YOU HAVE NOT THE *POWER* TO *STOP* ME. BEFORE ME YOU ARE AS A FLICKERING *CANDLE,* NOW TO RE-MAIN *FROZEN IN TIME* UNTIL I MIGHT HAVE NEED OF YOU AGAIN...

...TO POSSIBLY *RENEW* FROM THE ORIGINAL PAT-TERN THIS FORM I NOW WEAR.

...NO...

NO. I WAS PREPARED TO *DIE,* IF IT MEANT SAVING THE X-MEN, BUT NOT LIKE THIS. I WON'T LET YOU *DESTROY* THEM.

AND I *CAN* STOP YOU, *MONSTER!* I *DO* HAVE ONE WEAPON LEFT TO ME!

WHAT... DO... YOU... MEAN...?

YOU MAY HAVE FROZEN MY *BODY,* MONSTER. YOU MAY HAVE MADE ME A PRISONER, BUT I WON'T FAIL MY FRIENDS!

I CAN *STILL* SAVE THEM, EVEN IF IT COSTS ME *EVERY-THING!*

BECAUSE EV-ERYTHING IS WHAT I'M GOING TO *GIVE* YOU, CREATURE. ALL MY DREAMS, MY HOPES, MY LOVES, HATES, FEARS...

YOU WANTED TO BE ME, CREATURE? VERY WELL THEN.

BE ME!

NOOOO!!!...

YES!...

I'M ME! I'M JEAN GREY!! AND I'M ALIVE!!!

JEAN!

OH-h-h-h!

THE CRYSTAL!

THE POOR THING! SHE'S SHAKING LIKE A LEAF, DRENCHED IN SWEAT!

WHAT AN AWFUL EXPERIENCE TO HAVE SURVIVED!

IF SHE SURVIVED.

WHAT DOST THOU MEAN, REED RICHARDS?

YOU SAW IT ALL, TOO, HERCULES.

THAT ENERGY ENTITY DUPLICATED JEAN, TRIED TO BECOME HER.

THE QUESTION NOW CONFRONTING US IS: WHICH ONE OF THEM IS THIS?

OH, NO! PLEASE!

INDEED YOU WERE, JEAN. BUT I CAN SEE CAP'S POINT.
THAT LAST, DESPERATE EFFORT OF YOURS TO PREVENT THIS...PHOENIX FROM DESTROYING THE ONES YOU LOVED...
YOU MEAN... IT WORKED?
BETTER THAN YOU COULD POSSIBLY HAVE HOPED FOR, MISS GREY.
THE PHOENIX HAD DUPLICATED YOU DOWN TO THE LAST ATOM OF YOUR STRUCTURE.
IT HAD IMITATED THE PATTERNS OF YOUR BRAIN-WAVES SO PRECISELY THAT EVEN A TRAINED MIND-READER COULD NOT HAVE RECOGNIZED IT FOR WHAT IT WAS.
BUT YOU MADE IT DO MORE THAN THAT, JEAN. YOU MADE IT DUPLICATE YOUR INNER SELF.
YOU GAVE IT YOUR HUMANITY, JEAN.
YOU GAVE IT A SOUL.
AND, IN THE LAST MOMENTS, AS IT HOVERED BETWEEN LIGHT AND DARKNESS, UP THERE ON THE MOON, THAT'S WHAT MADE THE DIFFERENCE.
BECAUSE THERE'S NO FORCE IN THE UNIVERSE THAT CAN SUPPRESS THE SPLENDOR OF THE HUMAN SPIRIT. AND IT WAS THAT SPIRIT, EVEN IN DUPLICATE FORM, THAT WAS ENOUGH TO DEFEAT THE EVIL POWER OF THE PHOENIX.

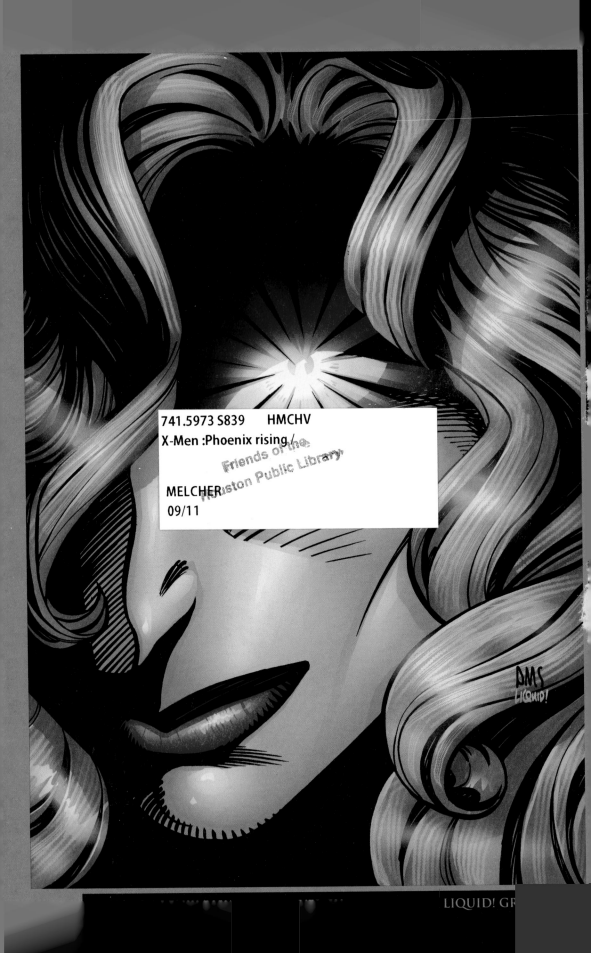
741.5973 S839   HMCHV

X-Men :Phoenix rising /

MELCHER

09/11

Friends of the
Houston Public Library